Self-Actualization and the Radical Gospel

Louis Roy, O.P.

A Michael Glazier Book

THE LITURGICAL PRESS
Collegeville, Minnesota

www.litpress.org

A Michael Glazier Book published by The Liturgical Press

Cover design by David Manahan, O.S.B. Photo copyright Marie Docher/Photo-Alto.

1   2   3   4   5   6   7   8

ISBN 0-8146-5107-0

Contents

Preface

As a priest and theologian, I would like to offer some clarifications as well as strong encouragement to those who take seriously the unique adventure that is their spiritual journey. In these pages I will argue for a reconciliation between self-actualization and the radical gospel, with a view to enhancing the reader's personal growth, while taking account of time, of successes and failures, and of various developmental factors. Although this book demands intellectual attentiveness and refers to good thinkers, I have decided not to write a scholarly work, but rather to present a series of well-organized reflections on a topic which is central to the lives of all Christians.

I am grateful to Rev. William Barry, S.J., Prof. John McDargh, Rev. Sebastian Moore, O.S.B., and Ms. Nancy J. Witting, who read the manuscript and made useful remarks about it. In addition to them, I would like to mention my Dominican brothers of Dover, Massachusetts, in whose house this book was composed. Their warm hospitality and their interest in the issue tackled here sustained me in my work.

Insofar as inclusive language is concerned, I alternate masculine, feminine, and neuter pronouns, so that what is said about an individual is true of both genders. However, in accordance with biblical language, God is referred to as "he."

Biblical quotations are from the New Revised Standard Version, published by Oxford University Press.

Introduction

The gospel is radical in what it requires of believers. Its intransigence explains the attraction, the fascination it has always exerted on those who seek the absolute. In fact, such people discover that despite enriching experiences and activities, life remains empty unless it is centered on a great cause or, more precisely, on a God whose goal for humanity merits the total consecration of their energies.

Apart from the believers who have staked their whole existence on the gospel and have not felt let down by God, there are many who have been disappointed by the social institutions or the churches, but who nevertheless are drawn to the gospel. These people wonder if Jesus and Christianity might still have something to say to them. Yet they are often repelled by the radical gospel, with its seemingly harsh and inhumane pronouncements.

There is a tension between two views of ethics. On the one hand, psychological humanism is based on self-affirmation, acceptance of one's limitations, moderation, and the search for a quality of life in the midst of globalization. On the other hand, the radicalism of the gospel emphasizes religious passion, self-transcendence toward the absolute, and generosity to God and others. These two tendencies are neither incompatible nor easily reconcilable. Although the tension is an uneasy one, it can be healthy if it leads to inquiry and reflection. We can gain much from engaging this tension in order to both understand and accept it.

Those different approaches will be explored in these pages. The first, typical of contemporary Western culture, is the drive toward self-fulfillment, impelled by psychology. (In this book, self-fulfillment, self-actualization, and self-realization will be treated as synonyms.) This ideal of self-actualization is ambiguous in relation to Christianity; that is, it can be either open or closed to the gospel. The second approach, found in the very heart of the Christian faith, is the radicalism of the gospel. This ideal has also proved rather ambiguous with regard to the development of the person. Therefore, we will attempt to interpret it correctly in its original setting, as well as in its theological significance.

The subject matter of this book is not so much an ideal as a reality which is dynamic, both objectively and subjectively. That is why we shall proceed dialectically. Showing the tension between self-actualization and the radical gospel, analyzing inadequate ways of appropriating each of these two sources of inspiration, and searching for an overall view that is at once psychological, philosophical, and biblical, we shall move toward a theological synthesis. While introducing permanent principles needed for a solution, this synthesis will prepare us for a return to the concrete problems that arise in putting the solution into practice.

Since many people have been led astray in the implementation of ideals, the first two chapters present defective forms of self-transcendence and self-actualization, and highlight what can happen when these tendencies are incorrectly construed. Given that these chapters quite naturally carry a negative tone, some readers may want to begin with chapter 3 and read them after going through the rest of the book.

Chapter 3 describes what occurs when the tendency toward self-realization is functioning well, that is, when it amounts to a wholesome kind of self-transcendence, which favors an enriching exchange with the surrounding reality. Chapter 4 underlines the intransigence of the gospel regarding the acceptance of painful situations and the renunciation of all that one possesses—and indeed of all that one is. It introduces the uncompromising demands of the New Testament and places them in their historical contexts. Chapter 5 explains how this radicalism draws its meaning from the reality of the kingdom of God, and discusses certain forms that it takes in today's world.

Chapter 6 builds on the philosophy outlined in chapter 3 and on the biblical insights set forth in chapters 4 and 5. It delineates the relations that can be established between self-actualization and the radical gospel. Opposed though these two outlooks may appear, nonetheless they can be synthesized by being placed within the framework of a Christian view of life. Finally, chapter 7 deals with the practical aspects of bringing about self-actualization within a religious perspective.

Chapter 1

Self-Transcendence Misunderstood

The ideal of self-transcendence expresses what is most noble in human nature, but in practice it is often characterized by defective forms, which can have serious consequences. This chapter identifies typical cases of a self-transcendence that is poorly understood and badly lived out, and gives a brief psychological profile for each case. I will call "altruism" this inadequate construal of our concern for others. This chapter deals with wrong ways of practicing self-sacrifice. In chapter 2, we shall come across a so-called "egotistic altruism," which reduces our concern for others to a minimum. Please keep in mind that throughout this book, altruism will be considered as a distortion of our genuine concern for others. As will be explained in chapter 3, both altruism and egotism are incompatible with authentic love of self and love of neighbor.

Ill-Considered Devotion

In *The Four Loves*[1] C.S. Lewis presents the case of a woman whom he calls Mrs. Fidget. He describes with black humor how the ill-considered dedication of this mother caused her family to be tense and unhappy. After her death, the entire family, including the dog, began to relax. Was Mrs. Fidget simply the victim of her unenlightened zeal? In reality, her devotion was not totally selfless. Her overwhelming generosity won admiration for her and prevented her children from criticizing her. She instilled in them a fear of disappointing her, a faultless person who was always right. Thus, they learned

---

[1] C. S. Lewis, *The Four Loves* (New York: Harcourt, Brace, 1960) 73–83.

to practice a sad and inauthentic sort of virtue, based on intolerance of weaknesses, whether their own or those of others.

Erich Fromm discusses a similar case in *The Art of Loving*.[2] He considers this kind of "disinterestedness" a neurotic phenomenon. Far from being a form of love, it betrays an incapacity to love others, appreciate their presence, and receive what they have to offer. This attitude is accompanied by symptoms such as depression, fatigue, lack of motivation in work, and failure in love relationships. Instead of attributing these symptoms to a defective way of loving, someone like Mrs. Fidget clings to her "disinterestedness," consoles herself with her immense efforts to give ceaselessly, and considers this disposition the trait of character that can redeem her, in the midst of all her problems. According to Fromm, such a person is paralyzed in her capacity for love and enjoyment, maintaining a blind hostility toward life and revealing herself to be self-centered, despite appearances to the contrary.

Fromm also notes the impoverishment that accompanies some people's experience of giving. Instead of envisaging a gift as a source of joy and an invitation to sharing, these people think that giving means "giving up" something, depriving themselves of it and renouncing it.

> They feel that just because it is painful to give, one *should* give; the virtue of giving to them lies in the very act of acceptance of the sacrifice. For them, the norm that it is better to give than to receive means that it is better to suffer deprivation than to experience joy.[3]

There is an unwholesome pleasure, an exaltation, almost a thrill in this form of giving, of thinking constantly of others, of feeling that one is needed. How heavily the recipients are burdened by this excessive generosity, this tense presence, and by the very gifts that are given! The giver does not let the receivers be autonomous, or provide the freedom they need to exist independently of the protective and monopolizing attention of the one who supposedly loves them.

In a similar way, many marriages fail when one of the partners tries to give everything to the other, to satisfy all the other's needs without asking anything in return. A person may sincerely believe that she is living out a great love, as she tries to ignore the extent to which her own expectations are going unmet. She may come to accuse her husband of ingratitude, or blame herself for the strain in their relationship. She may become vaguely aware that in systematically putting her hus-

[2] Erich Fromm, *The Art of Loving* (New York: Harper and Row, Perennial Library, 1956) 19.
[3] Ibid., 19.

band ahead of her, she is nourishing her partner's egotism. But she does not see clearly the conclusion that must be drawn, namely, that this altruism is not the right way to express love.

Another common error lies in not taking account of one's feelings, or distrusting them. A person may tell himself that love is fundamentally a question of will, that it cannot be based on what he finds pleasant, on what he desires. It is true that we cannot rely on passing emotions. But we should not forget that there are also enduring feelings. They are fundamental dispositions based on value judgments, which are not subject to change.[4] When positive sentiments of a transitory nature are lacking and one wants to maintain a conjugal relationship or a bond of friendship, it is important to consider the more profound inclinations and permanent value judgments that give orientation to one's life. If an individual fails to recognize and validate those dispositions, he may too quickly appeal to the force of will, thus falling into voluntarism.

Submission to Others

Unconditional submission to the will of someone else is another harmful way of dealing with our intimates. This attitude invites them to assume a position of superiority, from which it is easy to abuse their partner. As Gene Outka observes, the golden rule which says, "Do unto others as you would have them do unto you," is inverted to "Do unto others as *they* would have you do unto them."[5] This is again a matter of false love, an excessive deference to the desires of others, coupled with a lack of self-respect. Fearing conflict, one is unwilling to express displeasure or disagreement. The opinion of the other becomes decisive and final, since the need for approval and esteem is too great to risk criticism. By rendering oneself useful without causing inconvenience or conflict, one hopes to win appreciation and to receive concessions and favors in return. One also escapes the anxiety of making personal decisions.

This negation of self goes hand in hand with the notion that it is intrinsically virtuous to put aside one's own needs, to overlook the demands of one's emotions, to ignore inner thoughts. This renunciation allows some people to feel extremely good and thus to maintain a false self-esteem. In reality, the self that one tries to esteem is weak and dependent. Having as yet failed to reach maturity, the person is unable to

---

[4] Bernard J. F. Lonergan, *Method in Theology* (Toronto: University of Toronto Press, 1992) 30–41.

[5] Gene Outka, *Agape: An Ethical Analysis* (New Haven: Yale University Press, 1972) 275.

communicate adequately her vital drives, thoughts, and desires. Because she is incapable of clarifying personal perspectives, she cannot really enter into the viewpoints of others, even while superficially accepting them.

In the life of a married couple, the rationalization of this weakness takes the form of disastrous principles. For example, thinking it will make the other happy, one gives over to one's partner all initiative and decision-making. Thinking that loving means doing everything to please the other, one ignores one's personal tastes. Wanting only to be united with the beloved, one renounces an individual life with one's own interests, goals, and activities. The woman confines herself to the role of the submissive wife and absorbs herself in the tasks that flow from that role: cooking, housekeeping, care of the children, and so on. The man adopts the role of the breadwinner who has nothing to say about what goes on in the home. Such relationships often result in monotony, boredom, and dullness. The self that one would give to the partner becomes poor and insubstantial. In this way, one loses not only oneself, but also one's partner.

According to Wilhelm Reich,[6] masochism consists in turning against oneself the frustrated aggressiveness that cannot be directed toward external objects. A man's aggressiveness has been repressed along with his sexuality, which is also an object of fear. He is unable to channel the aggressive instincts. Hence, at times he may explode with anger, belying his ordinarily submissive and gentle nature. In actual fact, what his relatives and neighbors witness in him is "gentleness" based on a double hostility: hostility toward himself arising from the shame he feels for effacing himself, remaining silent, never criticizing, letting others make the decisions and solve the problems; and hostility toward those who profit from the submission he shows them.

Some people imagine that criticism of their ideas or behavior is a sign that they are not loved. They have little confidence in their own judgment. They are afraid of making mistakes, of being told (and therefore believing) that they are worth nothing. They exaggerate the importance of those who hold positions of authority. Hence, they cautiously follow the rules others make, never daring to think for themselves. They always obey the authorities, conform to the laws without reflection, and remain faithful to their obligations—without feeling free to reconsider them. Thus they sink into passivity and routine. Initiative and change are excluded. The great advantage of this easy and secure stance

---

[6] Wilhelm Reich, *Character Analysis,* trans. Vincent R. Carfagno (New York: Farrar, Straus and Giroux, 1972).

is that they avoid being blamed by their superego. Despite all these precautions, however, they cannot escape a more fundamental reproach, one that comes from their conscience: the awareness of having abdicated the better part of themselves.

Disguised	Despite appearances, the unhealthy modes
Self-Centeredness	of self-transcendence described thus far are forms of egotism. Although altruism seems

to express devotion, it often covers up ways of protecting ourselves against the eventual disappointments or sorrows caused by unrequited love. Sigmund Freud clearly saw that when we desire someone, we make ourselves dangerously dependent upon the one we love. We run the risk of being rejected by that object of love, or of losing it through unfaithfulness or death. Because of a deep fear of being hurt, we may have recourse to a radical solution: we make ourselves independent by displacing our highest value from being loved on to loving.[7] By blocking up our natural attraction to other people, altruism dramatically reduces our expectations and precludes the possibility of bereavement, thus turning out to be a preemptive strategy.

Altruism can also be an attempt to affirm our own self, by focusing on *our* peculiar ways of doing things for other people, with the result that we shut out their reality, namely, what they actually are and need. The tactics described above prevent communication and sharing. Defense mechanisms are set up to protect areas of weakness and confirm, in a bungling way, one's personal worth. While seeming to be centered on others to the exclusion of self, in actuality one does not understand and love others as they are.

The adoption of such disastrous attitudes can be explained historically by the pessimistic view of human nature found in many modern Western thinkers. Believing that the human being is fundamentally egotistic, these authors reflect in their writings a profound distrust of the self, sometimes to the point of self-contempt. Calvin contends that self-love engenders many vices, especially pride, and characterizes self-love and love for victory as "those most noxious pests."[8] Separating the supernatural from the natural, exalting grace without taking account of its incarnate aspects, they propose the artificial ideal of a pure and totally disinterested love, which expects nothing in return.

---

[7] Sigmund Freud, *Civilization and Its Discontents,* trans. James Strachey (New York: Norton, n.d.) 56–57.

[8] John Calvin, *Institutes of the Christian Religion,* trans. Henry Beveridge (Grand Rapids, Mich.: Eerdmans, 1989) bk. 3, ch. 7, §2 and 4.

It is important to note that this pessimism does not express Christianity at its best. From the High Middle Ages, for instance, consider the writings on friendship by Cistercian monks and by the Aristotelian Thomas Aquinas: one finds a philosophy of love in which all-important aspects receive a balanced presentation. The pessimism of the late Middle Ages has left a deep mark on Western culture. The characteristic psychological outlook of North Americans is a reaction against this pessimism—an optimism that goes too far in the opposite direction. This point will be further discussed in the following two chapters.

Many people today have abandoned this tense striving for an ideal that contravenes so many fundamental aspirations. Nevertheless, this attitude continues to be a permanent temptation, and numerous new converts to churches and sects succumb to this inauthentic behavior. That is why it is necessary to describe it and to show its defects. But before concluding this chapter, let us note a religious form of this falsely understood self-transcendence.

Self-Annihilation before God

In *God—In Fragments*,[9] Jacques Pohier uncovers the error of wanting to sacrifice everything to God in the belief that God is the Absolute, apart from which nothing else exists. This attitude is based on the idea of God as a totality, irrespective of his work of creation. Pohier rejects this attitude for an entirely different vision of God. Bestowing existence on what is not Godself, God creates finite beings. God does not choose to be so present to creation that it loses its own selfhood. Having placed the human being among other human beings, God does not want to be "Everything" to the human person.

Pohier notes that in mystical writings there sometimes occurs a transposition that is both subtle and unjustified. From the fact that creation is nothing without God, one deduces that creation is an illusion. Created realities are not illusions, however, unless one treats them as idols, expecting from them what one should expect from God. There is sometimes hidden pride in the determination to be indifferent to the attraction of created realities. In the last few centuries, Western monasticism oftentimes derailed as it negated human values. We find an example of that non-Christian attitude in Verdi's opera, *La Forza del destino*, where Leonora, thinking she has lost her lover, Don Alvaro, for good, resolves to lead the life of a complete hermit in a cave.

The mystics' dialectic of "all or nothing" can be experienced as a means of self-emptying in order to be exalted by the Father. The recom-

---

[9] Jacques Pohier, *God—In Fragments* (New York: Crossroad, 1986) 65–67 and 291–95.

pense that the person then expects corresponds to a desire touched by megalomania. Moreover, having renounced the world and accepted being nothing, the person no longer risks losing anything. He poses as being detached from human beings in order to be attached to God; in reality, this detachment is a means of avoiding suffering. It reflects a mentality more stoical than evangelical, as C. S. Lewis notes in *The Four Loves*.[10] Such a person does not recognize the play of finiteness, of imperfect human relations marked by hopes, disappointments, confrontations, and negotiations—all of which cause suffering. He does not accept the combination of light and shadow that makes life in the world both insecure and demanding.

A similar ambiguity is found in the limitless command of the gospel: "Be perfect as your heavenly Father is perfect" (Matt 5:48). This sentence stirs up an enormous sense of guilt in many Christians. Are they at fault because they are imperfect, limited, finite? Or are they guilty because they have consented to reprehensible attitudes and actions? In the first case, we are dealing with a global and primitive sense of guilt, which does not involve actual sinning; in the second, it is a question of a definite, realistic, and adult admission of guilt.

To accept our finitude entails that we recognize our need for other limited beings, and realize that our desire for them is good in itself, although the consequences of original sin make it difficult to act on such desire correctly. Therefore, nostalgia for a life open to the infinite and entirely given to God is ambiguous. Contrary to what Pohier says, however, as sons and daughters of the Father, we can be divinized by the Holy Spirit without fleeing human finitude. After all, that is precisely what Jesus experienced in his human life. He was the perfect Son accepting and living profoundly what is most simple, limited, and negative in the human condition. At the time of his temptation in the desert, he refused a messianic role that would have been prestigious and touched by megalomania. But if this was a temptation for that sinless man, how much more believers must expect to encounter it in their lives! We shall return to this issue at the end of chapter 6, when we tackle the question of happiness and finitude.

---

[10] Lewis, 167–171. He is nevertheless mistaken in attributing this stoicism to Augustine.

Chapter 2

Self-Actualization Misunderstood

Although it is natural to seek to realize one's potential, it is important to recognize how difficult that is. For example, according to the psychologist Abraham Maslow, less than one percent of the American people attain true self-actualization.[1] In striving for self-actualization, many misinterpret its true scope and are led astray. This chapter analyzes the defective forms of self-actualization that can result from a misdirected, though well-meaning and legitimate human tendency.

We shall speak of egotism, which is a *psychological* deviation, and of egoism, which is a *moral* deviation. The former naturally but not necessarily leads to the latter. The egotist is egocentric, self-centered, narcissistic, and yet does not necessarily intend to exploit others. The egoist is selfish, that is, self-interested at the expense of others, devoted to his own advancement without regard for the well-being of others.

The Search for Success

In Western societies, self-realization is often modeled on a vision of life that generally brings about disastrous results. This philosophy extols success for its own sake, and overlooks whatever ruse it takes to achieve it. Many people admire uncritically the individual who "makes it," despite the path followed. In the 1980s Colonel Oliver North, who made a mockery of the laws of the

---

[1] Abraham H. Maslow, *Toward a Psychology of Being*, 2nd edition (New York: Van Nostrand, 1968) 204.

United States in the Iran-Contra affair, was but one example of those heroes whose misguided courage aroused the admiration of the public.

The search for success is often manifested in efforts to acquire power and money. Such people find satisfaction in getting the better of others, in deceiving, manipulating, or intimidating them. They consider themselves more intelligent and stronger than others because they have this ability. Similarly, possessions can be symbols of personal worth. Houses, cars, clothing, the places one frequents, the people with whom one shares leisure time—all these advantages are enjoyed less for themselves than as signs that one is superior to others or belongs to an elite group. In short, the desire for power and possessions reflects the goal of attracting or even compelling the respect and admiration of others.

Let us also include in this category another type of person—the intense individual who finds self-realization through performance. Winston Churchill said that the adult who is in a hurry to excel was an unhappy child. This opinion is a little simplistic. More precisely, the adult who is in a hurry to excel was a child loved but conditionally, that is, loved in the measure in which he behaved well, performed good acts, and met with success. As a result, such an individual draws more pleasure and pride from noticing his own good acts than from seeing what those acts give to others.

Egotistic efforts to succeed often result in individual egoism and, on a larger scale, in the moral breakdown of society. We can draw up a long list of symptoms common to postindustrial societies: dishonesty and shady dealings in business and politics; an unscrupulous ambition in the workplace; an exaggerated emphasis on leisure-time activities and sports, along with a cultivated ignorance of socioeconomic problems; efforts to achieve sexual prowess; abortion, abuses of contraception, a low birth rate; the break-up of marriages considered statistically inevitable. What do these symptoms reveal? Efforts toward self-realization that abort, despite appearances, because these efforts are made at the expense of others and of the hierarchy of values. What one reaps ultimately is profound dissatisfaction, lack of self-esteem, and the absence of peace and joy.

In the contemporary West, the ideal of self-realization is too often misdirected, and used as an excuse to promote the egoism of individuals, special groups, and social classes. At the moment, we observe a new development: the group selfishness of the elders at the expense of the young generation, whose financial burden will be excessive when they begin to age, without health insurance or social safety net, and perhaps in an irremediably polluted environment. This egoism is as destructive of the individuals who succumb to it as it is of those who are its victims.

The Hunger for Immediate Experience

The unbridled pursuit of varied experiences, with all their new sensations and strong emotions, is a crude way of seeking happiness. In a world where the daily routine can engender boredom and the feeling that the individual is merely a cog in a gigantic machine, many people take no pride in their work. Many have not learned, either, to find self-worth in projects planned and carried out in cooperation with others. To ease their boredom, the young and not-so-young lose themselves in whatever self-gratification lies immediately at hand. One might say that only the sensation of living intensely proves to them that they actually exist. Their esteem for themselves depends on their capacity to satisfy their desires. They even pride themselves on inventing new desires and finding original ways of satisfying them.

This form of self-realization is childish because it confines the agent to the present moment, excluding those pleasures and joys that require a certain amount of preparation. Certainly, every person needs to renew her imagination and emotions by plunging into the here and now, to let her senses find pleasure in nature, and to take enough physical exercise to leave her healthily tired and relaxed. But while this sort of break from the serious tasks of the day contributes to a well-balanced life, immoderate pursuit of sensation destroys this equilibrium. Feelings experienced in this way only provide the illusion that personal worth can be increased by seeking and obtaining what one desires.

Dr. Viktor Frankl deplores the carelessness in fundamental education, which has failed to teach many young people an appreciation of the healthy tensions that accompany any worthwhile human enterprise:

> Man needs tension, challenge. If he is spared tension in this society of abundance and air-conditioning which is ours—a society where man is cosseted and spoiled by the softness of modern civilization—then it is by other means that he will find that tension. The truth is that we of the older generation have wanted to spare young people the healthy tensions which arouse vitality and which they need; and that is why many young people have turned to unhealthy forms of tension.[2]

The quest for immediate satisfaction makes one forget the importance of natural obstacles, which alone can give some tone to daily life. Too many people are not ready to sacrifice time and energy toward an eventual result. No doubt they have not experienced what it means to anticipate, savor, and prepare for a long-term objective. The tragedy is

[2] Viktor Frankl, *Un psychiatre déporté témoigne* (Lyons, France: Chalet, 1967) 169.

that they miss the only means for escaping the deadly boredom that drives them toward immediate gratification. In the long run, superficial excitement will lead to boredom and disgust. And prolonging leisure time does not reduce those negative emotions.

Who could be completely duped by this hoax? How can one not become aware, on some level, of submitting to the conventions and roles imposed by advertising and by the dominant mentality? Many people want to ignore that this is a collective lie, inasmuch as they have no hope that any other path will set them free. That is why they remain subject to an ideology of pleasure that seems to correspond well to experience. This anti-morality is a disguised morality; it inflicts guilt on people who feel they should have the audacity to satisfy all their desires. The right to happiness is expressed in this principle: "I *must* have what I want." If one does not get one's slice of the pie, one feels foolish, ridiculous, weak, less sharp than others. According to the morality of pleasure, living consists fundamentally in taking and consuming, but, in the final analysis, paying dearly for the purchases. One can easily understand why advertising purposefully encourages it.

The need for instant gratification entails particularly disastrous consequences in the matter of sexuality. Many people do not, in fact, have the patience to accept the rhythms and stages that render human relationships deep and enduring. They are all the more incapable of understanding and respecting the final purpose of their sexuality, which consists in expressing and strengthening the mutual love and support of two persons as they raise a family and take up social commitments.

The thirst for pleasure makes people demand more of certain types of activity than they can provide. "Greed is an impetus and insatiable craving, exceeding what the subject needs and what the object is able and willing to give."[3] Not only does one become a slave to a mass of artificial needs and encumbrances, but one tends ineluctably to abuse others. The compulsion to provide first and immediately for oneself destroys respect for what is most noble in others, namely, the capacity to share deeply and to establish lasting bonds. Dr. Igor A. Caruso gives a psychological explanation of this process:

> The thirst for emotion in the neurotic is the result of the conflict between two vital attitudes. The first consists in wanting to re-live an unexperienced love; the second, in wanting to prolong the delight of being loved. This desire to re-live an experience is revealed in a particularly serious form in a person who has been unhappy or abandoned in childhood; it results in an insatiable thirst to be loved—one, however, that is profoundly

---

[3] Melanie Klein, *Envy and Gratitude* (New York: Basic Books, 1957) 7.

hidden. This desire is especially acute in spoiled children and those who have been sacrificed to the egotistical love of their parents.[4]

As this quotation suggests, a person's insatiable need to experience emotion may be an effort to compensate for the fact that she has been insufficiently or badly loved. She is uncertain of herself, uncertain that she is acceptable and lovable. Fearing another disappointment, she avoids relationships where she might really be loved. Not believing in love, she contents herself with less, though perhaps seeking passionately this lesser object.

Moderate Egoism

In contrast to the people just described, we find the intriguing group of those who adopt a moderate type of egoism and who thereby cautiously pursue self-realization. Their education has endowed them with skills which permit them to enter harmoniously into relationships with others and to get interested in goals and undertakings requiring an investment of their time and energy. Think, for instance, of the brilliant creativity that is displayed in computer science as well as in the Internet business. Nevertheless, such people often achieve self-realization at the expense of others.

Moderate egoists generally function quite well. Most of them have had a relatively happy childhood. They have not suffered much and they are unprepared to suffer. Unless they are exceptionally ambitious, they do not take up major challenges; rather, they seize entertaining opportunities that will not involve too great a cost. They hold it as a self-evident principle that they have a right to happiness. Therefore, the misery of the poor does not keep them awake at night.

A certain subjectivism affects this personality type. When these individuals carry out well the tasks they undertake, they are more interested in efficient functioning than in the objective good to which the tasks are directed. Their primary objective is self-realization, understood as self-knowledge, self-confidence, harmony, spontaneity, creativity, personal growth, and the full development of their potential. The principal criterion of their action is psychological, pre-ethical. To the extent that this criterion truly influences their motivation, they are unlikely to love well, because in their love for another they love themselves first and foremost. They think that it is more important to be happy than to perform good acts for those around them. Thus their egotism turns into an egoism.

[4] Igor A. Caruso, *Psychanalyse et synthèse personnelle* (Paris: Desclée de Brouwer, 1959) 75.

Underlying this subjectivism, we find a simplistic kind of self-interest, which counsels, "Be egoistic; you yourself will be happy and others will only be the better for it!" A better rule of life might be phrased, "Do not think only of others, but think also of yourself inasmuch as a well-ordered self-love requires it." On the contrary, this subjectivistic self-interest says, "Think first and above all of your own personal interest," with the unavoidable outcome, "You yourself will be dissatisfied and others will only fare worse!"

Moderate egoists may follow this credo: "Be not egoistic, but simply egotistic, or self-interested, and without doing harm to others." But in reality, in cultivating their individual desires, they are likely to become blind to the harm they do to others. One cannot be at the same time egotistic and actively concerned for the good of others, least of all in a world where the poor tend to be segregated and kept out of sight. Prior to any moral consideration, these two attitudes are mutually exclusive on the psychological level. Even if one knows that individual interest, correctly understood, demands that one set limits to the misery of the poor, it remains true in the economic system that the excessive prosperity of some exists at the detriment of others.

Dr. Hans Selye, who has conducted experiments on stress at McGill University in Montreal, has tried to justify this morality of individual interest by talking about "altruistic egotism." He claims that the amalgamation of these two apparently contradictory principles provides guidance for individual behavior.

> Once he fully understands the philosophy of egotistic altruism, he is no longer ashamed of being an egotist. He admits to being self-centered and acts primarily for his own good; he greedily collects a fortune to assure his personal freedom and capacity for survival under the most satisfying conditions, but he does so through amassing an army of friends. No one will make personal enemies if his egotism, his compulsive hoarding of valuables, manifests itself only by inciting love, goodwill, gratitude, respect, and all other positive feelings that render him useful and often indispensable to his neighbors.[5]

Only a very small fraction of the world's population can put such principles into practice. Who, in fact, is capable of collecting "a fortune to assure his personal freedom"? And how can the masses who remain in poverty manage to live, according to Selye's view, "under the most satisfying conditions"? Far from being universal, as he proclaims it to

---

[5] Hans Selye, *Stress Without Distress* (Philadelphia: Lippincott, 1974) 115–16.

be while invoking "the unassailable laws of Nature,"[6] such a moral system justifies the wealth of creditors and puts a weapon into the hands of those who are defending their privileges.

The philosophy adopted by Selye has its letters of credit: it was also the philosophy of English author Thomas Hobbes, who lived in the seventeenth century, and it was taken up again by Sigmund Freud.[7] These two thinkers view the human person not as an essentially relational being, but as an individualist whose principal instinct is to preserve his biological existence and satisfy his desires. In a world where desirable goods are limited, individuals must coexist. This supposes that they respect rights, contracts, rules. Normally, these individualists would be totally egoistic. However, in order not to make too many enemies and to survive in society, they temper their egoism with a modicum of altruism. I am writing "egoism" because I find Selye's "egotistic altruism" indistinguishable from moderate egoism.

Selye, then, proposes a new version of that pessimistic philosophy. Like Locke,[8] however, he colors it with a moderate optimism. This philosophy underlies a part of the rationale for Anglo-Saxon democracies. It is essentially individualistic: it considers groups and societies to be associations of individuals who freely accept social contracts. In this framework, the continuity of human bonds always appears precarious; union and separation can succeed one another at a rapid pace. People do not trust engagements of long duration and easily justify the dissolving of relationships in marriage, family life, friendship, business and politics. As Christopher Lasch points out, "freedom of choice" means "keeping your options open."[9] Readers of Saint-Exupéry's *The Little Prince* could say that the moral principle has become, "I am not responsible for the rose I have tamed."[10] The idea of autonomy, which is not inherently bad, here retains the connotation of individualistic independence. Dependence and even interdependence are perceived as dangerous: to depend on others is to expose oneself to frustration and deception.

[6] Ibid., 115.

[7] See Thomas Hobbes, *Leviathan*, ed. Edwin Curly (Indianapolis: Hackett, 1994) and Sigmund Freud, *Civilization and Its Discontents*.

[8] See John Locke, *The Second Treatise on Civil Government* (New York: Prometheus Books, 1986) §11, 13, 15, 16, 19.

[9] Christopher Lasch, *The Minimal Self: Psychic Survival in Troubled Times* (New York: Norton, 1984) 38. For a fascinating documentation and discussion of such attitudes, see Robert N. Bellah and others, *Habits of the Heart: Individualism and Commitments in American Life* (New York: Harper and Row, 1985).

[10] Antoine de Saint-Exupéry, *The Little Prince* (New York: Harcourt, Brace, 1943) 71.

A More Complete Diagnosis

So far we have explored various forms of self-realization that end in at least partial failure. What is fundamentally lacking in these forms is attention to the *objective* aspects of self-transcendence. Very often, preference is given to lesser, materialistic goods, such as health, security, comfort, entertainment, and sexual pleasure. Blind to their more profound dimensions, these individuals deprive themselves of the spiritual aspect of reality and thus lose appreciation of life's rich value.

It is important to observe, however, that the reduction of the objective pole is accompanied by a caricature of the *subjective* pole. The self that attempts to realize itself without respect for the objectivity of others does not respect its own subjectivity. Jean Piaget clearly puts it:

> Through an apparently paradoxical mechanism whose parallel we have described apropos of the egocentrism of thought of the older child, it is precisely when the subject is most self-centered that he knows himself the least, and it is to the extent that he discovers himself that he places himself in the universe and constructs it by virtue of that fact. In other words egocentrism signifies the absence of both self-perception and objectivity, whereas acquiring possession of the object as such is on a par with the acquisition of self-perception.[11]

What is developed is not the whole of one's personal potential but rather a truncated subject, inattentive to its own questions, both intellectual and moral, and little adjusted to the demands of the unconscious. This limitation is often rationalized by means of reference to needs. A person tells himself, "I need this success, this experience, this entertainment, this thing, this person." In deluding himself, he turns a deaf ear to the important appeals trying to make themselves heard from the depths of his being.

In a psychologizing culture, materialism isolates certain psychological principles, good in themselves, in order to justify itself anew—this is called psychologism. The psychic functioning is separated from the moral sense. Certainly psychologists are right to put aside matters of morality for a time during the course of therapy so as to let the actual motivation emerge. But once these motives are recognized—an important aspect of self-knowledge—morality should be addressed. One must resist the conclusion that human beings *have to* base their decisions on

---

[11] Jean Piaget, *The Construction of Reality in the Child* (New York: Basic Books, 1954) xii. My attention was drawn to this text by Walter E. Conn, *Conscience: Development and Self-Transcendence* (Birmingham, Ala.: Religious Education Press, 1981) 104.

motives that are dominant in them. The motives themselves oftentimes need to be examined.

Such determinism is not to be found except in the case of a serious compulsion. Faced by differing motivations, which tend in various and even opposed directions, a normal person remains free regarding what action to take. Using the moral sense, which forms part of her intellectual equipment, she considers and compares the different actions she might choose. She then makes real choices, exercising true liberty in the face of its demands. All human freedom is obviously conditioned by motives. They are not unchangeable, however; they can, in fact, be modified as one becomes dissatisfied with their consequences, inquires into their true nature, and traces them down to their origins. Such a change takes a long time and calls for much hope.

Psychologism is a bad use of psychology. Concentrating *only* on the psychological advantages to be drawn from experience, it serves to justify the manipulation of the sense of good and evil. This manipulation becomes easier, the less one understands the profound responsibilities of the human being. Psychologism gains nothing from its one-sided view of reality. In fact, trying to separate psychological functioning from its ethical context creates problems even on the psychological level. It damages not only rationality, but even the psychological functions that interact with it. Lack of attention to moral responsibility can only impede self-realization, because concentrating solely on psychological satisfaction prevents feelings of deep moral satisfaction from playing their indispensable role.

Moreover, genuine moral responsibility, which allows for the overcoming of egoism, requires love of oneself. Regarding the presumably selfish individual, Erich Fromm asks, "Is his selfishness identical with self-love or is it not caused by the very lack of it?"[12] Whenever self-love is lacking, we can expect aberrations of both self-transcendence and self-actualization, in which the ego endeavors to assert itself through its accomplishments. Because it has been loved only conditionally, it craves recognition. In its obsession to give or to take—released in awkward expressions of either generosity or egoism—it seeks continually to prove its own worth to itself and thus it remains self-absorbed and contracted upon itself.

In this chapter, I have endeavored to show that misconstrued self-actualization can degenerate into an unsatisfying pursuit of individual accomplishments, experiences, and pleasures, with the aim of

---

[12] Erich Fromm, *Man for Himself: An Inquiry into the Psychology of Ethics* (New York: Rinehart, 1947) 128.

consolidating one's defective self-esteem. Our provisionary diagnosis has broached a subject that will be more lengthily unpacked in our next chapter, as we analyze components of self-transcendence such as pleasure, effort, values, intentionality, and the psyche. In so doing, we shall be in a position to demonstrate the complementarity between love of self and love of neighbor.

Chapter 3

The Tendency toward Self-Actualization

Notwithstanding the defective forms pointed out in the preceding chapters, the twofold concern for self-transcendence and self-actualization reveals the presence in the human being of a deep and positive dynamism. This chapter explores its strengths and implications.

A Consciousness Capable of Self-Transcendence

Despite the lack of conceptual precision that one finds occasionally in Abraham Maslow, this psychologist is a good guide in describing self-actualization. He remarks that it is gratifying to be drawn, interested, concentrated, and absorbed in a captivating experience. The experience might take the form of a film, a novel, a football game, or, more deeply, a sort of ecstasy—what Maslow calls a "peak experience." In his view, self-transcendence can occur whenever an activity causes you to forget yourself and go out of yourself to concentrate on a problem, an action, a subject, or a person. This transcendence in no way constitutes a diminishment or impoverishment; on the contrary, the more the self is transcended, the greater its strength and vitality become. According to Maslow, you realize yourself in transcending the self in favor of the dynamic reality that arouses your interest.[1]

This phenomenon can be observed in the productive process in which genuine artists are entirely immersed. Lionel Trilling quotes two great writers who testify to the self-forgetfulness that occurs in the midst of

---

[1] Abraham H. Maslow, *Toward a Psychology of Being*, 37, 105.

intense creativity. The first one is James Joyce, who declares, "The personality of the artist . . . finally refines itself out of existence, impersonalizes itself, so to speak." The second is T. S. Eliot, who avows, "The progress of an artist is a continual self-sacrifice, a continual extinction of personality."[2]

Maslow draws attention to a central element in human nature which makes self-transcendence possible. Besides the Freudian superego, a form of conscience that flows from the internalizing of parental authority, there is what Maslow calls "intrinsic conscience," based on our perception of our own nature to be respected, our destiny to be discovered and fulfilled, our abilities to be developed and employed, the truth that we must not betray, and the courage called for in some situations.[3] From this important remark we should deduce, more explicitly than the author does, that we transcend ourselves not only by getting interested in reality, but also by identifying and choosing those aspects of reality that our intrinsic conscience sees as having to be valued, respected, and promoted.

For Maslow, human autonomy consists in taking account of this intrinsic conscience, allowing oneself to be led in the first place by interior motives, that is to say, by one's own nature and sense of personal vocation, goals, and talents. Maslow emphasizes the necessity of maintaining a certain independence in the face of the environment and society, and in particular with respect to approval or disapproval, honors, rewards, accidental happenings, shocks, privations, and so on.

While insisting that each of us is autonomous, Maslow observes in the individual the capacity to become part of a greater whole. Rejecting a dichotomous manner of speaking, he unites in a hierarchical integration tendencies that are opposed to one another on a lower level: self-actualization and transcendence, awareness of intrinsic conscience and intense interest in exterior reality, inner ego-consistency and the desire to be part of a group wider than oneself, instinct and reason, heart and head, pleasure and duty, love of self and love of the other.[4] We shall examine some of these opposing tendencies.

The Role of Pleasure

No doubt because pleasure is by turns exalted and disparaged, it is hard to appreciate its true value. In a restricted sense, pleasure is physical. It accompanies the activity of the

[2] Lionel Trilling, *Sincerity and Authenticity* (Cambridge, Mass.: Harvard University Press, 1972) 7.

[3] Maslow, 6–7.

[4] Ibid., 34–35, 91, 139–40, 180, n.1, 212.

The Tendency toward Self-Actualization   21

senses. Thus we take pleasure in seeing, hearing, breathing, feeling, eating, drinking, touching, moving, and sexually uniting. Usually, however, we understand pleasure in more general terms—as the enjoyment, interest, satisfaction, gratification, joy, or peace that precedes, accompanies, or follows a positive experience. We speak, for instance, of the pleasure of giving and receiving, of the pleasure of travel, or even, with Roland Barthes, of the pleasure of the text.[5]

Although physical pleasure undoubtedly exists, still it cannot be attained in its pure state. Pleasure always takes on some kind of significance. The intellect situates pleasure in a meaningful context. The individual who pursues immediate pleasure often does so not only for enjoyment, but also to enhance his self-esteem thanks to the resoluteness, audacity, and creativity he employs in satisfying his needs. The human being does not find physical pleasure apart from the meaning he attaches to it. The film *The Last Tango in Paris* illustrates the impossibility of experiencing a purely physical pleasure, which would imply forgetting all the rest.

The fact that we ascribe some meaning to a pleasure (even when we say that we want it for itself) shows that we feel a need to justify it. To justify it is to place it in a context in which things take on meaning. When it acquires meaning, physical pleasure becomes allied with pleasure in the broader sense. For example, we derive pleasure from taking part in various sorts of meals, from lunch quickly eaten during midday pause to dinner at an excellent restaurant, or a party at home, or a wedding banquet. The various significations attached to the meals complete the pleasure we get from eating well.

For Aristotle, pleasure is something that accompanies a virtuous (or excellent) activity. Pleasure is neither the goal nor the objective of the activity; rather, it is an encouragement that flows from the activity. It is not the fruit, but the flower. The goal is the global meaning that one gives to one's life; the objective is the value of the activity itself, the good it represents. Pleasure is the joy felt in doing what has significance because it is estimable and well oriented. In accord with his Greek perspective, Aristotle finds deep satisfaction in the noble and beautiful character of the deed that is done.[6]

The objective and subjective sides of human action are thus conjoined. When a psychologically and morally healthy person says of an activity, "That interests me," she unites the objective and subjective

---

[5] Roland Barthes, *The Pleasure of the Text*, trans. Richard Miller (New York: Hill and Wang, 1975).

[6] Aristotle, *Nicomachean Ethics*, trans. Martin Ostwald (Indianapolis: Bobbs-Merrill, 1985) bk. 1, §8, and bk. 10, §1–6.

aspects. She is concerned about both the value in question and the gratification that accompanies the experience. In a text that is worth citing at some length, the French philosopher Henri Bergson explains eloquently the living relationship that naturally exists between objectivity and subjectivity, creation and joy.

> Wherever there is joy, there is creation; the richer the creation, the deeper the joy. The mother beholding her child is joyous, because she is conscious of having created it, physically and morally. The merchant developing his business, the manufacturer seeing his industry prosper, are joyous—is it because money is gained and reputation acquired? No doubt, riches and social position count for much, but it is pleasures rather than joy that they bring; true joy, here, is the feeling of having started an enterprise which goes, of having brought something to life. Take exceptional joys—the joy of the artist who has realized his thought, the joy of the thinker who has made a discovery or invention. You may hear it said that these men work for glory and get their highest joy from the admiration they win. Profound error! We cling to praise and honours in the exact degree in which we are not sure of having succeeded. . . . But he who is sure, absolutely sure, of having produced a work which will endure and live, cares no more for praise and feels above glory, because he is a creator, because he knows it, because the joy he feels is the joy of a god.[7]

This joy is not the preserve of people who are exceptionally successful. Any person who believes in God and who tries to maintain a certain quality of life can participate in the divine creativity and experience of joy.

The Role of Effort

The role of pleasure, then, consists in accompanying and sustaining creative acts, sources of good. However, neither the apprehension of value nor the presence of pleasure is enough to guarantee that the required action will follow. Effort is also needed to fulfill a function that completes that of pleasure.

When we are only barely motivated, or torn by contradictory motives, or when the value to be found can be attained only at the price of sacrificing great pleasures, we act only with immense effort. And in some circumstances, strenuous effort is called for. Nonetheless, we are never well served by voluntarism, that is, by granting excessive importance to the will, as if its exertions might be meritorious in themselves. To avoid voluntarism, effort should be associated with, and supported by pleasure understood in the broader sense. Moreover, obstacles ought

---

[7] Henri Bergson, *Mind-Energy: Lectures and Essays* (Westport, Conn.: Greenwood Press, 1975) 29–30.

not to be seen as detrimental, but as opportunities to become a deeper and wiser person.

Freud speaks of the importance of knowing how to move from the pleasure principle—focused on what is immediate—to the reality principle—focused on the long term. He correctly considers the reality principle as safeguarding pleasure over a long stretch of time.[8] Effort becomes less arduous if one knows that it may lead to gratifications which matter more than the pleasures one must sacrifice. As Pascal wrote, "One does not give up pleasures except for other greater ones."

All in all, pleasure is not meant to be an end in itself. Paradoxically, it is diminished when given priority over the good to be accomplished. On the other hand, it is as sane and normal to want pleasure as to want the flower that signals the coming of the fruit, the good action. When a motivated person functions well, the satisfaction experienced is compensation for the effort made to accomplish the good. It is the sign of both the excellence of the person and the value of what is brought into being.

Unfortunately, some people imagine that the presence of pleasure discredits the authenticity of love. Cynics and idealists, whose positions are at opposite poles, nevertheless agree that there is no love in an action that is pleasant. Cynics say, "We are egotists in every respect because in everything we do we seek only our own interest." Idealists make the claim, "True love is only what is costly, requires effort, and calls for much courage." The two groups have a negative understanding of pleasure, of the satisfaction one finds in performing good actions, and, in the last resort, of human nature itself. They cling to the false idea that love supposes absolute gratuity. But even in the Holy Trinity, the divine Persons, while not having to acquire anything, enjoy one another in their exchanges. Furthermore, God has created human beings capable of entering into relationships where they both give and receive. We are so constituted that we cannot fail to obtain something whenever we love others sincerely and wisely.

The Hierarchy of Values

As quoted in chapter 2, Maslow points out that very few people attain self-actualization. He offers two reasons to explain this disappointing fact. First, "the conviction that man's intrinsic nature is evil or dangerous"; and second, the fact that "humans no longer have strong instincts which tell them unequivocally what to do, when, where and how."[9] Insofar as the second reason

---

[8] Sigmund Freud, *Civilization and Its Discontents*, 26, 29.
[9] Maslow, 204.

is concerned, we may ask, are such "instincts" always constructive? Cultural or religious tendencies of a legalistic kind sometimes succeed in convincing and firmly guiding groups, and even whole societies. Still, one pays an excessive price for this, namely, a diminution of critical rationality.

Notwithstanding the reservation I have just expressed, the problem posed by Maslow is a very real one. In extremely complex, postindustrial societies, where the effects of our actions are more difficult to evaluate than they would be in an agrarian society, there is clearly a loss of objectivity. The kaleidoscopic screen of the mass media outruns our capacity for assimilation. The absence of a consensus regarding values and customs brings about a mixture of contradictory phenomena: rigidity and lawlessness, obstinacy and manipulation, intolerance and laissez faire. One way or the other, reflection and dialogue seem almost nonexistent. A large portion of the population loses sight of the importance of what takes place in the public sphere. People become alienated from their own work. In the private sphere, many try to compensate for the lack of satisfaction they find in their work by being absorbed in instant pleasures.

This does not mean that the private sphere remains inviolate. In his book *The Minimal Self,* Christopher Lasch rightly sees the "minimal or narcissistic self," which is characteristic of our time, as projected in "a world of mirrors, insubstantial images, illusions increasingly indistinguishable from reality." It is uncertain of itself, of the external reality, and of the boundaries between itself and that reality. Lasch argues that "the fantastic mass-produced images that shape our perceptions of the world" have brought about "the replacement of a reliable world of durable objects by a world of flickering images that make it harder and harder to distinguish reality from fantasy." The consequences are "submission to expert judgment, . . . distrust of their own capacity to make intelligent decisions."[10]

Part of the answer to this difficult problem lies in acquiring the hierarchy of values. Bernard Lonergan provides the following explanation of the scale of values.

> We may distinguish vital, social, cultural, personal and religious values in an ascending order. Vital values, such as health and strength, grace and vigor, normally are preferred to avoiding the work, privations, pains involved in acquiring, maintaining, restoring them. Social values, such as the good of order which conditions the vital values of the whole community,

---

[10] Christopher Lasch, *The Minimal Self,* 30, 19, 29.

have to be preferred to the vital values of individual members of the community. Cultural values do not exist without the underpinning of vital and social values, but none the less they rank higher. Not on bread alone doth man live. Over and above mere living and operating, men have to find a meaning and value in their living and operating. It is the function of culture to discover, express, validate, criticize, correct, develop, improve such meaning and value. Personal value is the person in his self-transcendence, as loving and being loved, as originator of values in himself and in his milieu, as an inspiration and invitation to others to do likewise. Religious values, finally, are at the heart of the meaning and value of man's living and man's world.[11]

For Lonergan, then, inferior values allow superior values to emerge in the following order: vital, social, cultural, personal, and religious. To realize one's potential amounts to actualizing one's values and skills, beginning with the vital ones of the body, including also membership in communities and society, the quest for meaning in culture, excellent functioning as a person, and openness to the divine.

But how can we succeed in respecting this scale of preferences? In part, the answer is religious, and dependent on perspectives and motives discussed in the following chapters. Another part of the response is philosophical; it has to do with the fact that the human being has the capacity to be truly interested in reality. Let us continue to take up the philosophical aspect of this question.

Intentionality and the Psyche

The Creator has implanted in us a fundamental dynamism that enables us to know, love, and transform. Following Brentano and Husserl, philosophers call this dynamism "intentionality," that is, the ability to tend toward (*in-tendere* in Latin), to open ourselves to reality. Now, this reality comprises not only things, animals, and people around us, but also ourselves. To know, love, and transform ourselves is as spontaneous and legitimate as to know, love, and transform others. Therefore, our intentionality includes both self-realization and self-transcending toward reality. As I transcend myself, I realize myself as a loving subject.

Intentionality implies a twofold transcendence of self, as the two meanings of the verb "to transcend oneself" suggest. First, one transcends oneself by going out of oneself in order to know and love persons and other beings as they are, and not as one imagines or desires

[11] Bernard J. F. Lonergan, *Method in Theology*, 31–32.

them to be. This requires the exercise of an exact and balanced judgment, carefully and correctly evaluating situations in order to achieve real good for other people. That is the *objective* aspect of intentionality, which consists in self-transcendence.

Human intentionality also wants to transcend itself in the sense of achieving excellence. And here we have the *subjective* aspect of the same dynamism, which amounts to self-realization. Every individual endowed with a certain measure of vitality possesses in some way a taste for excellence. Once basic needs are satisfied, as Maslow points out, the vital person desires to face more significant challenges, which are more satisfying, give meaning to daily life, and allow her to grow as a human being.[12]

To achieve self-realization, one must take into account both one's intentionality and one's psyche. Intentionality is the source of questioning and reflection. It is open to the external world, seeking to understand and evaluate it. It looks to exact knowledge, well founded value judgments, and the discernment of lines of action that respect other people in their environment. This is to say that intentionality has a moral dimension in its deepest sense. While intentionality is the principle of unlimited opening to the whole of reality, the psyche appears as the principle of limitation. Since the psyche is in touch with our bodily needs, it fulfills the function of mediating them to our intentionality by way of affects and images.[13]

On the one hand, without a healthy psyche, intentionality tends to be disembodied, cold, legalistic, willful, and even destructive. When people cannot count on a sound psyche, their behavior gets distorted, no matter their good intentions. On the other hand, if intentionality operates as it should, it strives to establish an alliance and an equilibrium with the psyche. By making wise decisions regarding one's lifestyle, intentionality helps the psyche to flourish in a relatively harmonious atmosphere enabling positive perceptions and feelings. Moreover, the psyche can accept frustrations, which intentionality should negotiate—not impose in a dictatorial manner. Thus, in any well-balanced person there is a dynamic tension between intentionality and the psyche.

[12] Maslow, 25. For a more thorough analysis, see Louis Roy, *Transcendent Experiences: Phenomenology and Critique* (Toronto: University of Toronto Press, 2001) ch. 9, section entitled "Intentionality and Transcendence."

[13] My understanding of intentionality and psyche is dependent upon Robert M. Doran, *Psychic Conversion and Theological Foundations: Toward a Reorientation of the Human Sciences* (Chico, Calif.: Scholars Press, 1981) 28–29.

**Love of Self and
Love of Neighbor**

The philosophical and psychological principles set forth in this chapter lead to the conclusion that far from excluding each other, love of self and love for the other are mutually complementary.[14]

We have seen in chapters 1 and 2 that neither altruism nor egoism promotes self-realization. In fact, on the one hand, to renounce one's pleasure systematically in favor of others' pleasure constitutes a sacrifice that inevitably engenders frustration, attempts to obtain some compensation, resentment, and even hostility. On the other hand, consistently putting one's own pleasure before that of others brings only bitter satisfaction to even the least lucid individual.

Paradoxically, selflessness and egotism have the same roots: both are misguided ways of valuing oneself, either by one's misplaced generosity or by one's numerous acts and pleasures. In each case an important aspect of the self is ignored. A self-denying person ignores his wishes by not acknowledging his legitimate needs, his valuable ideas, his profound aspirations, and the unique way he could realize himself as a human being. An egotist ignores that inclination in himself which desires to love the other for what she is, and to promote in society values that are independent of his own immediate interests. Both the one who systematically sacrifices himself and the one who remains consistently self-absorbed are victims of mistaken strategies, associated with false notions of what it means to love others and oneself. By contrast, as Aristotle remarks, enlightened self-love consists in loving the highest part of one's soul.[15]

A sound philosophy of love rests on intentionality. It is manifested in the tendency to ask appropriate questions: Who is this person? What are the problems and procedures of this group? Is my information correct? Is the action I contemplate worthwhile? Will this act prove to be a good means to the end? What attitudes are suitable in this situation? This kind of questioning shows that it is natural to pay attention to reality, to people, to the good to be sought, and to steps to be planned.

Now, the reality that must be understood, loved, and transformed includes the self as well as the other. Therefore, to love is neither always to concentrate totally on others nor always to be centered on oneself; it is to alternate between these two complementary operations. The

[14] On the compatibility between self-love and benevolence, see Joseph Butler, *Five Sermons Preached at the Rolls Chapel* (Indianapolis: Hackett, 1983), sermons 4 and 5, "Upon the Love of our Neighbor" [= sermons 11 and 12 of the complete edition, entitled *Fifteen Sermons Preached at the Rolls Chapel*].

[15] Aristotle, *Nicomachean Ethics*, bk. 9, §8, see §7–9; see also bk. 8, §3–6.

alternation ought not to be misconceived as an alternation in terms of loving: one does not sometimes love others and sometimes love oneself. Rather, the alternation is a matter of accents in attentiveness. On the one hand, we must turn toward the external reality that requires commitment, toward the true good of other people, toward the institutions and practices which sustain a just and harmonious social life. On the other hand, we must face our own reality, know our potential, discover the basic line of our destiny, and choose activities that are suitable to our personality.[16]

Erich Fromm points out what we can gain from knowing how to give:

> In the very act of giving, I experience my strength, my wealth, my power. This experience of heightened vitality and potency fills me with joy. I experience myself as overflowing, spending, alive, hence as joyous. Giving is more joyous than receiving, not because it is a deprivation, but because in the act itself of giving lies the expression of my vitality.[17]

Notwithstanding its insightfulness, Fromm's description of the pleasure received in giving does not go far enough. This pleasure is really more than the agreeable feeling of one's power, vitality, and wealth. The satisfaction derived from giving is deeper, because it is also linked to intentionality—viewing the other as different from me, identifying the needs and desires of the person I love, and responding with both affection and intelligence to the profound value that I discern in the other. This is precisely what sincere love wants for its partner: that the other might taste in turn the joy of paying attention to me, truly understanding me, and loving me with his whole heart and mind. For the sake of oneself and the other, there is an objective interest in inviting the other to grow in love.

And yet, despite the irreplaceable role that it plays in sustaining and rewarding the effort that love requires, this joy is more than enthusiasm aroused by functioning well, even in love. Joy derives from a good act, and the act is seen to be good if its object is worthwhile. If one attends to what intentionality at its best is really pursuing, one notices that love finds its raison d'être beyond the satisfaction of loving. To love and be loved is to want to love and be loved *because it is good*, because it fits within a human relationship. Love is justified first and above all by virtue of the good it seeks.

---

[16] In *Love, Human and Divine: The Heart of Christian Ethics* (Washington, D.C.: Georgetown University Press, 1994), Edward Collins Vacek offers a balanced treatment of self-love and love for others, which is more detailed than the one I give here.

[17] Erich Fromm, *The Art of Loving*, 18–19.

In interpersonal love the growth of the people involved is paramount. The satisfaction of loving accompanies the actualization of this good and contributes to the development of each person. Effort is seen as an ally of satisfaction, while both effort and satisfaction are subordinated to the emergence of this good. It is not natural to love and help people first and above all in view of the joy one will derive from it. On the contrary, to be fully human consists in welcoming with gratitude the joy of loving and of acting justly because that joy helps me to love and act justly. From the Aristotelian viewpoint adopted in this chapter, the pleasure of contributing to the advancement of a person or a group is obtained as a consequence inseparably linked to that good.

To return to the rather optimistic quotation from Erich Fromm, it should be mentioned that he does not take into account the dramatic situations in which most human beings often find themselves. Under suffering, many find it extremely difficult not to break down. They need to draw upon resources which are usually considered religious. In the trials of life, love develops and takes on its full meaning only if it is taken up into a larger whole of a transcendent kind, which makes it possible to cope with the question of evil. This broader context will be sketched in the following chapters.

Chapter 4

The Radical Gospel: Historical Setting

What we find in the New Testament on self-realization appears totally opposed to the humanistic plan for self-development. It is a matter of what the exegete Thaddée Matura calls "gospel radicalism," defined as "the most absolute requirements of Christian existence." Matura understands radical to mean what goes against ordinary wisdom, "what departs from habitual behavior and customs, what is extreme, hard, trenchant, abrupt and demanding."[1]

Gospel radicalism is incarnated in many forms: to be poor, chaste, faithful to one's marriage partner, to become a wanderer dependent on the hospitality of others, to choose Christ and the gospel over one's intimates, to castrate oneself for the kingdom of heaven, to renounce power, to welcome the alien, to be open to sinners and those excluded from society, to forgive seventy times seven times, to do good to one's enemies, to take the last place, to accept insults, calumnies, arrest, trial, loss of material goods, torture, and death.

It is impossible, of course, for any one person to respond to all these demands at the same time. Some of them are, in fact, incompatible—for instance, fidelity to one's marriage partner and celibacy for the kingdom. On the other hand, how could one be a Christian without manifesting in one's life some form of this radicalism? In Church history, each generation of believers has been creative in this regard. Every period, every Christian community, and every person has been invited to identify the forms of radicalism that should be actualized in the following of Christ.

---

[1] Thaddée Matura, *Suivre Jésus* (Paris: Cerf, 1983) 23–24.

Sometimes the disciples of Jesus have become radical as a result of having taken bold initiatives; sometimes they have become so simply by having consented to the implications of their religious commitment.

The New Testament asks believers to perform costly acts, to adopt courageous attitudes, and not to shun painful situations. However, it would be a mistake to think that these actions, attitudes, and sufferings have religious value in and of themselves. To understand why the gospel is so revolutionary, we must examine its various contexts.[2]

Mission and Opposition

One of these contexts is that of mission. Sent by Jesus, the disciples became itinerants who traveled with the least possible goods. Thus, they were dependent, because they needed the hospitality of those who did not share their Christian faith. "Take no gold, or silver, or copper in your belts, no bag for your journey, or two tunics, or sandals, or a staff; for laborers deserve their food" (Matt 10:9-10). These missionaries are the "little ones" spoken of in Matthew 10:42 and with whom Jesus identifies himself in Matthew 25:31-46. It is to them that kindly non-Christians gave food and drink; it is they who were welcomed when they were strangers, who were clothed when they were naked, and who were cared for when they were ill; it is they who were visited in prison.

The content of their preaching caused hostility and created a situation of opposition, resulting in conflicts, insults, calumnies, arrests, trials, flagellations and death (Matt 10:16-20). Poverty for the sake of the gospel is explained by these two situations—itinerancy and opposition. A disciple was poor either because he left his possessions behind in order to go from village to village proclaiming the Good News, or because his goods were seized by adversaries who rejected the Christian message. Moreover, when certain members of the Jewish or pagan community recognized Jesus as the savior and others did not, the new Christians sometimes lost the love of their close relatives. Thus came painful divisions and denunciations within families and towns (Matt 10:21-22, 34-39).

This complex situation of preaching and conflict can be seen in the life of St. Paul, who felt responsible for and united with all human beings, since God calls every person to be part of the body of Christ. Nothing can be understood about Paul without first grasping his missionary desire to make the word that liberates spread worldwide, and to provide support to all in the process of conversion and transforma-

---

[2] My reading of the Beatitudes has been heavily influenced by Jacques Dupont, *Les béatitudes* (Paris: Gabalda, 2nd ed., 3 vols., 1958–73).

tion. He explained this several times, notably in chapter 2 of the first letter to the Thessalonians. He wrote that he did not seek to please people or to receive honors. His dedication to the recipients of his letter was complete. "So deeply do we care for you that we are determined to share with you not only the gospel of God but also our own selves, because you have become very dear to us" (1 Thess 2:8).

His attention was focused on one thing: making known "the Good News," "the word of God" (vv. 2, 4, 8, 9, 13). His motivation was eschatological; it looked toward the community of the last days. "For what is our hope or joy or crown of boasting before our Lord Jesus at his coming? Is it not you? Yes, you are our glory and joy!" (v. 19).

Invitation to the Marginal	Ending the marginalization of those in Israel who were considered impure constitutes another context of self-transcendence. The

evangelists saw Jesus not as a prophet who kept himself pure by avoiding contact with the unclean, but rather as the Holy One of God, who cured them by communicating his own purity to them. The first stage of salvation brought by Jesus consisted in bringing back "the lost sheep of the house of Israel" (Matt 10:6; 15:24) in order to restore the whole nation to its pristine unity. Note the list of those who enter the kingdom first, or to whom the Good News must be preached first: the sick, the dead, and the lepers (Matt 10:8); the blind, the lame, the lepers, the deaf, the dead, and the poor (Matt 11:5; Luke 7:22); the poor, the captives, the blind, the oppressed, and all those who will profit by "a year of grace" (Luke 4:18-19); the poor, the crippled, the blind, and the lame (Luke 14:21).

Giving priority to the "unclean" could not help but raise problems for Jesus. The Pharisees and the scribes complained, "This fellow welcomes sinners and eats with them" (Luke 15:2). The difficulty came from the fact that his welcome was not preceded by any request for purification. For instance, in the case of Zacchaeus (Luke 19:1-10) Jesus did not immediately require acknowledgment of sin, and he himself initiated the contact. He also took the initiative in inviting himself to dinner at the home of a public sinner, thus fulfilling a deep aspiration on the part of Zacchaeus who "was trying to see who Jesus was." In sharing a meal with this sinner, who was excluded by the religious authorities, Jesus offered him the possibility of communion with God. The incomparable presence of Jesus—rather, of God, who saves through the humanity of Jesus—gave Zacchaeus the motivation he needed to be converted.

During the Pauline mission to the pagans, a similar problem arose. Many Jews, even among those who believed in Jesus, did not admit that Christianity (which was then viewed as a branch of Judaism) could exempt from the mosaic regulations pagans who had been converted to Christ. The openness that Jesus had shown to sinners who were Israelites, and the welcome he accorded to pagans who had not embraced Judaism, furnished other reasons for some leaders to attack the first Christians. We find an echo in the parable of the workers in the vineyard (Matt 20:1-16). Projecting onto God a human idea of justice which is not sufficiently aware of divine generosity, certain of the Jews who had worked for centuries in the vineyard of the Lord found it unreasonable that the recently arrived pagans should receive the same wages. Furthermore, Jesus did not hide the fact that the blunted spirituality of Israel would have disquieting results: "The last will be first, and the first will be last."

Stating that the kingdom of God was open to the unclean and to the pagans, Jesus aroused opposition in those who believed that the frontiers of religious purity and moral observance should be impenetrable to such people. It was not that Jesus abolished these frontiers. On the contrary, his calls for repentance make clear that he did not practice any complicity with sin. Far from diminishing the difference between good and evil, he accentuated it. But having taken this difference to an extreme (in the Sermon on the Mount), Jesus showed that the kindness of God cancels out evil, as he drew near to sinners and loved them deeply. This radicalism on the part of Jesus had a way of frightening the just. How, indeed, can one love sinners without collusion? How can one find the strength to enter onto this dangerous and unsatisfactory path? Fears like these prompted many to reject the message of Jesus.

Moreover, the priority Jesus accorded to the poor and his announcement of a reversal of social situations quite naturally led most of the rich to perceive the Good News as bad news. "How hard it is for those who have wealth to enter the kingdom of God! Indeed, it is easier for a camel to go through the eye of a needle than for someone who is rich to enter the kingdom of God" (Luke 18:24-25).

Luke points out that certain Pharisees, who loved money, made fun of the warnings of Jesus about the incompatibility of serving God and wealth (16:10-15). While Jesus did not condemn the possession of money, he nevertheless denounced the prestige and the illusory security associated with money, as can be seen in the episode of the poor widow (21:1-4), the parable of Lazarus and the rich man (16:19-31), and the story of the wealthy landowner who amassed great stores of grain just before his death (12:13-26).

It is easy to understand why the priority Jesus gave to the marginalized, the `pagans, and the poor aroused the indignation of the orthodox and constituted a challenge for the disciples.

Relationships within Communities

Relationships within Christian communities constitute another context of self-transcendence. The disciples were invited to prefer the last place to the first (Luke 14:7-11). Unlike the heads of nations, religious leaders were told not to make their power felt, but instead to become the servants of others (Matt 20:20-28). The greatest in the kingdom, Jesus said, will be the little one, the child, the youngest, the one who serves at table (Matt 18:1-5; 19:13-15; Luke 22:24-27).

Christian brothers and sisters should be concerned about the sheep that has gone astray; they ought to correct one another and pardon one another from the bottom of their hearts—not seven times, but seventy times seven times (Matt 18:10-35). Among the petitions in the "Our Father," this duty of forgiving is the only one that Jesus returns to and insists upon (Matt 6:9-15). Its importance is thereby highlighted.

Matthew emphasizes another situation where love requires some delicacy: not to occasion the fall of a little one, while taking care not to fall oneself (Matt 18:6-9). Paul discusses this problem in chapter 8 of his first letter to the Corinthians. On the one hand, he defends the freedom of the Christian to eat food sacrificed to idols. Those who believe in the one God know well, of course, that idols do not exist outside the minds of those who venerate them. On the other hand, Paul points out that, for the weak, an occasion of falling might be caused by this freedom. Paul concludes, "That is why, if food can be the cause of a brother's downfall, I will never eat meat anymore, rather than cause my brother's downfall" (v. 13). It is in this context that he urges his fellow Christians: "Do not seek your own advantage, but that of the other" (1 Cor 10:24; see v. 33).

Suffering, Attitudes, and Behavior

Another form of radicalism consists in the sufferings that Jesus invited his followers to undertake. Addressed directly to disciples ("Blessed are *you*") who found themselves in difficult situations, the Beatitudes in Luke's Gospel proclaim that those are blessed who are poor, hungry, mourning, hated by others, rejected, insulted, and defamed for the sake of the Son of Man (compare with 1 Cor 4:9-13). The Beatitudes and the curses (Luke 6:20-26) as well as Mary's canticle (Luke 1:46-55) announce a reversal of fortunes linked to the advent of a new world.

In Matthew 5:3-12, the Beatitudes have more to do with attitudes and behavior. There, Jesus proclaims blessed the poor in spirit, the meek, those who are waiting to be comforted, those who hunger and thirst for justice (namely, to accomplish God's will), the merciful, the pure of heart, the peacemakers, and those who are persecuted for the sake of justice.

The six antitheses that follow (Matt 5:21-48) urge the disciple to go as far as possible in respecting others: not to become angry with one's brother or insult him, but rather to be reconciled with him; not to look at another man's wife to desire her, but to take even drastic measures to avoid sin; not to repudiate one's wife or marry the rejected wife of another; not to swear at all, but to keep one's word; not to resist an evildoer, to turn the other cheek; to give the thief one's coat and to give generously to those who ask; to love one's enemies, to pray for one's persecutors; and not to be content with loving only one's brothers and those who love in return. Matthew's antitheses uncover that which people would ignore: the roots of violence, be it against one's brother, one's wife, the person that one sexually desires, the contender in court, the enemy, the persecutor, or the stranger.

Finally, passages from the Gospels that do not form part of such organized wholes also point to radical acts to be accomplished. Thus, in response to the question, "Who is my neighbor?" Luke 10:29-37 cites the example of the good Samaritan, a foreigner who acted as a neighbor to the man who had been robbed, beaten, and left for dead on the road from Jerusalem to Jericho. In the same way, Jesus suggests to a person giving a banquet that his guests be the poor, the crippled, the lame, and the blind, who will not be able to repay; these will, in fact, be the ones whom God will bring together at the great dinner in the kingdom (Luke 14:12-24). Or again, following the requirement of conjugal fidelity, repeated by Matthew in chapter 19, Jesus evokes the possibility of celibacy for the sake of the kingdom of heaven.

We have sketched numerous forms of Christian radicalism found in various situations in the New Testament. It remains for us to complete this inventory by asking what meaning such radicalism might have in our present world.

Chapter 5

The Radical Gospel: An Interpretation

Having drawn attention to the numerous forms of radicalism found in the New Testament (especially in the Synoptic Gospels and St. Paul), we must go further and attempt to answer the following questions: What motivation makes radicalism possible? To whom does Jesus address his calls for self-denial? How can one live out nonresistance and forgiveness?

Motivation

Certain expressions that appear in the context of self-denial reveal the motivation underlying radicalism. When Jesus urged his disciples to undertake difficult acts of renunciation, he gave the following reasons: "because of my name" (Matt 10:22); "for my sake" (10:39); "for my sake and for the sake of the gospel" (Mark 8:35); "for the sake of the kingdom of heaven" (Matt 19:12). In the face of what Jesus represented, the Good News that he proclaimed, and the kingdom of God that was present in his person and in his actions, the radical words he spoke find their context. It was the urgency of the desire to devote oneself to the kingdom of God that explains the fact that the disciple had nowhere to lay his head and renounced going first to bury his father or to say farewell to those of his household (Luke 9:57-62).

Exegetes point out that the kingdom of God is the leitmotif of the Gospels, that this theme is found in all the literary genres, and that all the other motifs are clarified by this theme.[1] The message Jesus brought

---

[1] See Michel Gourgues, *Jésus devant sa passion et sa mort* (Paris: Cerf, 1979) 27.

is the "Good News" (the gospel), closely linked to the coming of the kingdom of God (Mark 1:14-15). The Good News is announced first and foremost to the poor (Matt 11:5; Luke 4:18), as Isaiah predicted (Isa 61:1). The poor, be it noted, include tax collectors and sinners, who recognize more easily their need for a physician than people in good health (Matt 9:9-13). The sinful woman, because she is aware that her numerous sins have been forgiven, shows much love (Luke 7:35-50). Thanks to their faith, public sinners such as tax collectors and prostitutes will precede the priests and the elders into the kingdom of God (Matt 21:23-32). They welcome with more truthfulness and depth the healing and liberation offered by Jesus.

Moreover, the kingdom implies the tearing down of walls and barriers that separate human beings, often in the name of God. Such was the case with Israel in the time of Jesus. He himself went out to the rejected and touched those who were afflicted with ills attributed at that time to the presence of various demons. When the Pharisees claimed that Jesus cast out devils by the prince of devils, Jesus replied that it was impossible for the house of Satan to be thus divided against itself. He added, "But if it is by the Spirit of God that I cast out demons, then the kingdom of God has come to you" (Matt 12:28). The kingdom of God is realized, then, in the action of Jesus. His cures indicate that the kingdom is already present. In the same way, one can view acts of radicalism as signs of the kingdom. As Matthew 19:12 suggests, certain believers decide to be celibates "for the sake of the kingdom of heaven."

There was strong opposition raised in reaction to the proclamation and realization of the kingdom of God. Jesus was the first to experience enormous resistance to his message and his way of life. Indeed, his arrest, condemnation, and crucifixion issued from the rejection of that message and way of life. However, insofar as Christians misunderstand the message and fail to imitate its practice, the world honors them. On the other hand, as soon as they take seriously the radicalism of the gospel, they become the target of defamation, and means are taken to overcome their influence:

> If the world hates you, be aware that it hated me before it hated you. If you belonged to the world, the world would love you as its own. Because you do not belong to the world, but I have chosen you out of the world—therefore the world hates you. Remember the word that I said to you, "Servants are not greater than their master." If they persecuted me, they will persecute you (John 15:18-20).

Radicalism is motivated by the desire to imitate this master whom one admires, to resemble more and more this friend and brother, who shows the way that leads to life.

The greatness of Jesus, which believers can imitate, amounts to defying the consequences of one's commitment. It consists in maintaining one's orientation, and in declaring that it is willed by God. It means going so far as to assert that there is no salvation outside of this way (Acts 4:12). It is to proclaim courageously the necessity of conversion for all, from the smallest to the greatest. Thence comes the deadly antipathy of those who do not believe Jesus was the mouthpiece of God. They think that the established order is threatened by the inflexible allegiance of his disciples to "truth," and they fear that attempts may be made to overthrow an unjust state of affairs which benefit those who oppose the gospel.

Jesus proclaimed, "It is more blessed to give than to receive" (Acts 20:35). Yet giving is associated with suffering. Reflecting on the life of Jesus, one cannot fail to be struck by his heroism. Unfortunately, many are content to admire it from a distance, without wondering about its source. The foundation of this heroism is the coming of the kingdom. Because God comes to reign, a new horizon appears and great things become possible. Faith in the kingdom of God, which was realized in the action of Jesus, led both Jesus and his disciples to strikingly radical acts, attitudes, situations, and sufferings.

Judged abnormal by all purely human standards, these actions take on a convincing meaning in the Christian context. It is a matter of making visible the immense generosity of God, which is the substance of the great charter of the kingdom. As Helmut Thielicke stresses, in the logic of the New Testament the divine gift precedes the radical commands: "we are not given something to do without first being given something."[2] He explains:

> The sermon on the Mount says to us: a future has been *given* to you. . . .
> In the name of that future we can afford to be radical and absolutely
> straight, without allowing ourselves to be pushed off on the diagonals of
> the parallelogram of power or to tack on a zigzag course. In other words:
> first comes the future and then the unconditional demand, the straight
> line, the right course—and not the other way around.[3]

Given this extraordinary future, the believer wants to express the kindness, the tenderness, the mercy, the unparalleled love of God for all human beings. By becoming one with the least interesting, the most deprived, and the most hardened of human beings, she *takes the initiative*

---

[2] Helmut Thielicke, *Life Can Begin Again: Sermons on the Sermon on the Mount,* trans. John W. Doberstein (Philadelphia: Fortress Press, 1963) xiii.

[3] Ibid., xiv.

of showing the signs of the kingdom. In order to share with others the Father's extravagant love as manifested by Jesus, she is ready to accept actions, attitudes, situations, and sufferings that seem irrational, humanly speaking. All this is to be explained by the fact that the disciples have received the light of faith, which allows them to look at people and events through the eyes of Jesus.

Faith in the reality of the kingdom, then, makes possible great love for one's neighbor. This same faith, likewise, allows one to accept evil. The Cross of Jesus sheds light on the failures, defeats, sufferings, and absurdities one undergoes. Any negative experience can become fruitful if it is lived with love, in union with Jesus.

> Very truly, I tell you, unless a grain of wheat falls into the earth and dies, it remains just a single grain; but if it dies, it bears much fruit. Those who love their life lose it, and those who hate their life in this world will keep it for eternal life (John 12:24-25).

One finds here the religious motive, which sustains the gift of self for others. One is willing to sacrifice oneself for the gospel, for the people one loves, and even for one's enemies, because one believes it will contribute to the salvation of the world. Gospel radicalism finds its ground and dynamism in the very way God wants to liberate humankind.

Those to Whom the Message Is Addressed   To whom are the appeals to radicalism addressed? The vocabulary indicates that a good number of such challenges are addressed to all Christians: "all," "whoever," "the disciples," "the crowd." Precepts of a general nature are valid for everyone, because they sum up what the particular precepts set forth in detail. Thus, every disciple must follow Jesus, carry one's cross, and lose one's life. However, there are many different ways of fulfilling this condition, which is common to all.

That is why many radical acts are not imposed on all; they variously apply to particular situations and circumstances. Foreign missionaries, for example, are itinerant, renounce material goods, and live far away from their families. Also, persecutions occur regularly in the course of the history of the Church. In some countries, for example, not belonging to the ruling party may mean that one is deprived of interesting studies and a promising career; dissent can result in incarceration in a psychiatric hospital or prison, forced labor, or exile. Activities on behalf of human rights can usher in a situation where an individual is molested, beaten or tortured. In regimes of the extreme Left as well as of the extreme Right, many Christians of living faith have paid dearly for their commitment to truth and justice.

Nevertheless, an adequate interpretation of the radical gospel rules out a number of alternatives. First, the Sermon on the Mount is not a set of laws literally imposed on everyone. As was pointed out at the beginning of chapter 4, some of those laws happen to be incompatible with others. It would be a mistake to fancy that they are binding precepts for all Christians. According to this inadequate construal, they would be supernatural commands as universal as Kant's categorical imperatives, based on practical reason.[4]

Second, a similar error consists in stating, after Luther, that the pronouncements of Jesus are at once morally inescapable and unattainable. As such, their role would be to expose the believers' sinfulness, so that they may give up their confidence in human works and entrust themselves to divine grace.[5] In partial agreement and disagreement with Luther, we would maintain that *with the grace* imparted by Christ, the requirements of the radical gospel are in a great measure implementable.

Third, Max Weber drives a wedge between an ethics of conviction *(Gesinnungsethik)*, illustrated by the Sermon on the Mount, and an ethics of responsibility *(Verantwortungsethik)*, represented by the practice of those who must run human affairs. This highly influential German sociologist maintains that there is total opposition between the former, essentially pacifist, and the latter, based on violence (or the violent squelching of violence). Being idealistic, "acosmic," and confined to the realm of personal relations, the first kind of ethics can be adopted only by saints and may serve as an inspiration. Weber's resigned acceptance of the second kind of ethics, the only kind viable on the collective plane, follows from his tacit assumption that there is no divine grace operative in the people who make political decisions. All the same, he acknowledges the fact that sometimes politicians combine conviction with responsibility—which seems to rebuke the fundamental opposition he has set between the two kinds of ethics.[6]

Having dispensed with grace, Max Weber offers a secularized version of Luther's view, with its separation of the inner man from the outer man. Weber rightly sees, however, how self-deceptive is the attitude of those who cultivate generous feelings and good intentions at the neglect of social analysis and realistic behavior. The radicalism of the gospel has nothing to do with a vague romantic inspiration that would occasionally call for impotent forms of social protest.

[4] Immanuel Kant, *Grounding for the Metaphysics of Morals,* trans. James W. Ellington (Indianapolis: Hackett, 1993) 402, 421, 429–34, 440, 444 (marginal numbers).

[5] Martin Luther, *Christian Liberty,* ed. Harold J. Grimm (Philadelphia: Fortress Press, 1985) 11–12.

[6] Max Weber, *Politics as a Vocation,* trans. H. H. Gerth and C. Wright Mills (Philadelphia: Fortress Press, 1965) esp. 45–55.

Fourth, another way of bypassing Matthew's Sermon on the Mount—and the even more demanding Luke's Sermon on the Plain—is to declare that they are an obsolete ethics, an ethics which was viable only during the period of eschatological crisis which followed the resurrection of Jesus. In contrast to the first disciples of Jesus, who expected an imminent end of the world and thus could afford being heroic for a little while, we would be entitled to see the words of Jesus as beautifully expressing a mere ideal. Inspirational though it could be, this dream would never be concretized into practical decisions, particularly over a long period of time.

Fifth, contrary to what Thomas Aquinas teaches, it is an anachronism to see the pressing appeals for self-abnegation found in the Gospels as counsels specifically addressed to members of religious communities whose life is more perfect by being structured along the requirements of obedience, poverty, and chastity.[7] The New Testament nowhere suggests a distinction between precepts for all believers and counsels for the religious. Countless lay Christians have adopted forms of radicality that are different from religious life and no less demanding. Furthermore, New Testament's ethics is not elitist: all are called to practice its exigencies, with a mixture of success and failure.

If we look closely at the details of the radical gospel, we can observe that certain of Jesus' appeals—such as love, forgiveness, and purity of the heart—are obviously universal. Others are particular, for instance celibacy: "Let anyone accept this who can" is the challenge Jesus flings down in Matthew 19:12. Whether universal or particular, however, these radical points all reflect real practices in New Testament times. It is necessary, then, to envisage them, in all their diversity, as the many *possibilities* offered by the kingdom—possibilities which become *actualities* thanks to divine grace. "The content of these requirements is often clear-cut and definite; the way to live them in the concrete is left, as a disquieting challenge, to creative invention."[8]

For example, what are the requirements regarding the sharing of goods? Such sharing seems to be required of everyone, at least in the sense that according to the tradition of most churches, Christians should give a part of their income to their parish, which must then care for the poor. But certain groups go so far as to hold all their goods in common. The Acts of the Apostles (2:44-45; 4:32-37) recounts how this integral sharing of goods allowed the leaders to distribute them according to the

---

[7] Thomas Aquinas, *Summa Theologiae* II–II, q. 186, a. 1 and a. 2.
[8] Thaddée Matura, *Le radicalisme évangélique* (Paris: Cerf, 1978) 198.

needs of the members of the community, so that no one was in want. This is a possibility offered by the kingdom, which quite a few perceive as a goal to be realized in their own lives. To the rich young man who had kept all the commandments, Jesus said: "If you wish to be perfect, go, sell your possessions, and give the money to the poor, and you will have treasure in heaven: then come, follow me" (Matt 19:21). Note the appeal to personal freedom: "If you wish to be perfect." This appeal meets a desire to do or to be more: "What do I still lack?" (Matt 19:20). But there are times when the desire can prove too weak: "He went away grieving, for he had many possessions" (Matt 19:22).

Similar differences are found concerning commitment to the mission. Although not all Christians are called to be apostles in the way that St. Paul was, all should offer and direct their daily actions to facilitate, directly or indirectly, the conversion to Jesus Christ. This collaboration in the Christian mission is carried out in interpersonal relationships, and in the physical and organizational activities that support them. A hierarchy of values unites communion with God, human relations, and the rest of our activities, so that in the economy of the incarnation nothing is despised. What is asked of all Christians is to act wholeheartedly and bring a high quality to their daily tasks, as humble and routine as they may be.

The gospel bids us to do more than what is strictly necessary, and to follow appeals that lead in different directions. For example, in prayer, acceptance of intimacy with God is a costly way of living radicalism. "Whenever you pray, go into your room and shut the door and pray to your Father who is in secret; and your Father who sees in secret will reward you" (Matt 6:6). In a world where people are accustomed to receiving strong daily doses of sensory stimulation, it takes a courageous resolve to accept the austerity of solitude and silence.

A radical stance is also displayed in commitment to social justice. Postindustrial societies tend to isolate and overlook those whose personality and lifestyle do not manifest the general mood of optimism: members of the lower economic classes, the unemployed, those on public assistance, the handicapped, the ill, the elderly, the dying, and so forth. To break down this barrier requires sacrifice. To respect profoundly the small as well as the great, to put those who are in dire necessity ahead of those with less need, to struggle against attitudes based on contempt and prejudice—all this runs counter to what most human beings think and do. Moreover, if someone is serious about staying informed about economic injustice and its causes, and about putting pressure on political leaders through various channels of communication, this individual becomes unpopular. Pope John Paul II brought criticism upon himself when he called attention to the debts of poor nations and the exploitation of the Third World by capitalist countries.

Gospel radicalism is thus a risky and less traveled road. It is "the way of God" (Acts 18:26). One must go forward with confidence and inventiveness in following him who is "the way, and the truth, and the life" (John 14:6). It is for each person to discern, among the many types of radicalism that the kingdom makes possible, which ones are suited to one's nature and circumstances. Each person and each Christian community must determine for themselves what reality corresponds to the call of God.

Nonresistance and Forgiveness

To complete this discussion of radicalism, let us consider two often misunderstood passages of the Sermon on the Mount. The first of these passages concerns nonresistance:

> But I say to you, Do not resist an evildoer. But if anyone strikes you on the right cheek, turn the other also; and if anyone wants to sue you and take your coat, give your cloak as well; and if anyone forces you to go one mile, go also the second mile. Give to everyone who begs from you, and do not refuse anyone who wants to borrow from you (Matt 5:39-42).

Yet Jesus himself seems not to have put into practice what he recommends. Struck by one of the high priest's guards, he did not turn the other cheek, but replied, "If I have spoken wrongly, testify to the wrong. But if I have spoken rightly, why do you strike me?" (John 18:23). And when Paul, the great apostle of Jesus Christ, was struck on the order of the high priest, he did not mince his words: "God will strike you, you whitewashed wall! Are you sitting there to judge me according to the Law, and yet in violation of the law you order me to be struck?" (Acts 23:3).

No intelligible interpretation of this gospel text can be made if we consider the precept to be universal. The clear practice of Jesus and Paul contradicts it. But one can view that saying of Jesus as a possibility of the kingdom, to be discerned and put into practice whenever necessary. At certain moments in interpersonal relationships and in the life of groups, one should turn the other cheek. Jesus and Paul did so under other circumstances—and in an absolute manner at the time of their martyrdom. In situations that are deteriorating, the enforcement of strict justice may become unrealistic, and the acceptance of suffering through love may be the only solution. Sometimes, for the very good of those who are attacked and of those who attack, we ought to defend the former (including ourselves) by word and action. At other times, for the good of the attackers and with the hope that they will reconsider, we ought to accept abuse, but without masochism or indignity.

Assessing such situations requires prayer, in order that we not lose sight of the radicalness of the gospel. We must have confidence that the Holy Spirit will instill the wisdom "so that you may discern what is the will of God—what is good and acceptable and perfect" (Rom 12:2), and the strength to put it into practice.

In the "Our Father," a petition says, "Forgive us our debts, as we also have forgiven our debtors" (Matt 6:12). And Jesus adds: "If you forgive others their trespasses, your heavenly Father will also forgive you; but if you do not forgive others, neither will your Father forgive your trespasses" (Matt 6:14-15). This passage seems to suggest that the pardon granted by God is conditioned by the pardon people grant to one another. And surely this impression raises questions.

Moreover, a parable recounted by Matthew seems to confirm the conditional character of divine pardon. After proclaiming the necessity of forgiving seventy times seven times, Jesus tells that terrible story in which an official to whom the king has remitted a large debt refuses to act in the same way toward a servant who owes him a small amount. Learning of this ungrateful and pitiless behavior, the angry king has the official arrested and handed over to the torturers until he pays his whole debt (Matt 18:21-35).

At first sight this is a poor image of God: a being who goes back on his pardon and exercises justice with severity and cruelty. But to think so would be to miss the point of the parable. Rather, the emphasis is on the logic that carries the believer from the God-given forgiveness to the forgiveness granted among human beings. Not only does divine pardon precede human pardon, but there is an enormous disproportion between the debts remitted. Listening to the parable, we are urged to recognize the inconsistency of our behavior when, ignoring all that God has forgiven us, we refuse to forgive the little wrong that others have done us. To admit this inconsequence is to open ourselves to conversion and salvation. That is what the parable is intended to effect in us.

But what is to be said about the conclusion? Its harshness is meant to produce in us a salutary fear, the fear that we might eschew forgiveness altogether because we (not God!) are harsh. Obviously one need not interpret the parable to the letter. Educated Christians may hold, with Thomas Aquinas, that God does not change his mind, does not put people to the torture, and does not refuse anyone his pardon. Problems with pardon do not arise on God's side, but on ours.

God wants to pardon and never withdraws his offer. But human beings can refuse this gift. They have been created free; they can say yes and they can equally well say no. In refusing to forgive others, they say no to the divine offer of pardon by rendering themselves incapable of receiving it. Thus, the two stages in the parable—the debtor-creditor's incoherence and God's angry response are actually an indivisible whole. Because of the incarnation, people who do not forgive the other members of Christ's body put themselves into a psychological position where they cannot really accept the forgiveness of Christ. It is precisely this disastrous situation that is to be feared, because it is psychologically and spiritually much worse than physical torture.

The parable as well as the "Our Father" unveil very high stakes. What can you do if you do not feel capable of pardoning another "from your heart" (Matt 18:35)? We must view the act of pardon within the context where grace and time do their work. If, under the shock of the blow received, we begin by rejecting the very prospect of forgiving, the parable of the two sons can encourage us. It reminds us that the one who first refused to obey his father later changed his mind and did what his father commanded (Matt 21:28-31). The Holy Spirit alone can grant us the capacity to forgive. That grace acts over the course of time and adapts itself to our limitations.

The important thing is to be willing to engage in a process of reconciliation. God asks no one to adopt an unsustainable rhythm. Hence the importance of taking one step at a time and of distinguishing different phases—not necessarily chronological—in a journey of forgiving whose length varies enormously depending on individual backgrounds.

The first phase is the decision not to take revenge. This resolution is all the more difficult to make when one is troubled by not having defended oneself adequately in the first place. To strike back and to score a few points might have the advantage of restoring a better self-image. But one must renounce both the pleasure of taking revenge and the illusion of strength that accompanies it.

A second phase consists in being fair to the person who is in the wrong. If our work or a particular situation requires objectively that one collaborate with or render a service to that person, one should do it, however difficult it may be.

Another step to take is to talk to the person and make clear what happened. If this dialogue has some chance of success, one should risk it. Jesus recommends such action in a passage that precedes (and balances out) the one calling for forgiving seventy times seven: "If another member of the church sins against you, go and point out the fault when the two of you are alone. If the member listens to you, you have regained that one" (Matt 18:15). What follows in the text suggests the possibility of involving other people. In the absence of the aggressors, pardon can be given in silence; at other times it should form part of a process of confrontation. In the life of a married couple, for instance, only some combination of frank dialogue and forgiveness can ensure a fidelity that is maintained without damage to their psychological health.

Up to this point we have not discussed emotions. That is because forgiveness involves much more than emotions, namely, acts, as we have just seen. We can enter into the process of pardoning long before we feel positive toward those who have hurt us. But feelings are nevertheless important, and the experience of indignation, revolt, powerlessness, hatred, antipathy, resentment, contempt, or the desire for retribution can be overwhelming. We must admit that we are unable to govern our emotions directly. They can be altered by new perceptions, by a change of outlook or atmosphere. It is enough to desire that negative feelings may pass. Nothing more is asked of us than to be open to the grace that gradually operates in us. Jesus alone cures our wounds—sometimes quickly, but generally slowly. "By his wounds you have been healed" (Isa 53:5, as quoted in 1 Pet 2:24).

Prayer is equally indispensable. We have to pray for ourselves, that we become capable of forgiving. We must also pray for those who have wronged, offended or injured us, that they learn to love. Thanks to prayer, painful events that have marked us will come to be placed in a Christian context, and will thus be relativized. This context is well presented by St. Paul, when he writes that God has set reconciliation in motion in the world:

> So if anyone is in Christ, there is a new creation: everything old has passed away; see, everything has become new! All this is from God, who reconciled us to himself through Christ, and has given us the ministry of reconciliation; that is, in Christ God was reconciling the world to himself, not counting their trespasses against them, and entrusting the message of reconciliation to us (2 Cor 5:17-19).

This chapter has offered an interpretation of radicalism. In closing, let us return to the important idea that the radicalism of the gospel makes sense only in relation to the kingdom. The different forms of renunciation are subordinated to the presence of the Father in his incarnate Son, to the action of God renewing humanity through the life of Jesus. In a world where injustice so often prevails, only the Cross is the answer to the problem of evil. It expresses God's response to the negative side of human history. But the Cross exists for the sake of the resurrection: the negative is assumed by the positive, which encompasses it. Although the role of the negative escapes us to a considerable extent, faith allows us to counter it thanks to radical actions in our concrete circumstances.

The entire Bible conveys intense faith and unrestrained love of life. The Jewish *shalom* is based on the fact that God wills and brings about the good of his people. In the same way, it is out of gratefulness for the life given and given again by the Creator that the Maccabees accepted martyrdom (1 Macc 7). The positive appears also in the Beatitudes, when

Jesus declares "happy" those who suffer for the kingdom. The Wisdom of Solomon addresses God as "O Lord, you who love the living" (11:26). Comparing himself to the good shepherd who gives his life for his sheep, Jesus sums up the meaning of his mission in these words: "I came that they may have life, and have it abundantly" (John 10:10).

Chapter 6

Toward a Synthesis

Having explored self-realization and the radical gospel, we can tackle our central question: are these ideals incompatible, or can they coexist, indeed fuse with one another? To ensure that we are not going to outline a facile reconciliation between these two ideals, let us begin by listening to St. Paul.

> Let no one deceive you with empty words, for because of these things the wrath of God comes on those who are disobedient. Therefore do not be associated with them. For once you were darkness, but now in the Lord you are light. Live as children of light—for the fruit of the light is found in all that is good and right and true. Try to find out what is pleasing to the Lord. Take no part in the unfruitful works of darkness, but instead expose them (Eph 5:6-11).

We cannot ignore the fact that Christian radicalism rules out the way in which, *in fact,* self-realization is generally carried out. In light of the drastic prescriptions of the Sermon on the Mount and of the urgings of Jesus to deny oneself, take up one's Cross, and give up one's life, it is clear that the gospel demands a heroism at the opposite pole from current wisdom. Its message unmasks the superficiality of self-realization as it is ordinarily understood. The loftiness of Christianity, expressed in Jesus' command, "Be perfect as your heavenly Father is perfect" (Matt 5:48), brings out by way of contrast the restricted horizon and the limitations of humanism.

Paradoxically, this collision between the ideal of the gospel and current wisdom is illuminating. It is through contact with what is great and beautiful that human reflection becomes aware of its deviations and begins to listen to its profound aspirations. Thus, in our chapter 2, the light of Christian revelation has helped us to uncover what is lacking in the tendency toward self-contentment.

Given the demands of the New Testament, some people conclude that they must abandon the concern for self-fulfillment altogether. In chapter 1, we have exposed the illusions that this stance often carries. Christians are entitled to trust that God calls them to develop, with the assistance of grace, all that is positive in human nature. And yet we must add that self-actualization, when pursued with religious faith, has a different meaning, much more profound than the purely secular one. Self-actualization is integrated into a much richer context—God's dream for humanity.

From the Ego to the Self

We have noted that in modern times the West has emphasized the intrinsic worth of the individual. This is a sound achievement since it has fostered respect for the rights of the person. But an insistence on individual importance can too easily slide into the cult of the ego. When that happens, the ego becomes an absolute, which evaluates everything in relation to itself. Then the "ego trip" that characterizes adolescence is prolonged indefinitely.

If egoism constitutes a deformation of a moral kind, which hurts other people, the psychological egocentrism of which we are speaking is also at fault and requires an explanation. This egotism betrays an anxiety concerning oneself. It is a preoccupation that derives from the fact that a fundamental desire has yet to be satisfied: the desire for proof that the author of the world and of life cares deeply about me and loves me passionately, despite all my mistakes and imperfections.

Christianity does not consider the ego an illusion. It recognizes the need to be valued as a demand written in the human heart by the Creator. All people want to prove themselves. Think of the immense satisfaction babies feel when they first grasp things and manipulate their physical environment. Throughout and beyond one's accomplishments, each person wishes (and legitimately so) to be seen as special, unique, and irreplaceable. Lasting peace derives from the knowledge that one is not only loved, but also lovable.

While taking up all that psychology and ethics have to say about the increase of self-esteem, Christianity offers much more. The value of a person is based on the fact that God has created her and offered her two great gifts: freedom in Jesus Christ and a share in the trinitarian life. Just because it is founded on the love of God, self-esteem does not become an extrinsic characteristic. The love of God, in fact, allows a person to internalize this esteem and make it her own.

It remains true, however, that every truly religious person cannot be content to live within the limits of the individual self. If we reflect seriously on self-realization, we have to ask what "self" we are talking about. Maturity consists in shedding the illusion of a purely individual ego so as to rejoice that one is integrated into a greater whole. For the Christian tradition, what is illusory is not the ego, but the isolated ego, namely, the ego that fails to understand that the experience of belonging is constitutive of the self.

It is here that the distinction between the ego and the self proves useful.[1] The ego is the aspect that feels, protects, and promotes one's individual identity. The self is the aspect that wants to participate in an ensemble greater than itself. When a person is persuaded of being placed on this earth to live out, in suffering and joy, a profound mystery of love, he ceases to be obsessed by the "me" and he has already begun to explore the religious universe. He also escapes the trap of construing the passage from ego to self as a self-enlargement that is in fact mere ego-aggrandizement. One can enjoy the illusion of becoming a fuller self without being actually committed to other people and consequently without really participating in a broader self.

Each one of us is essentially relational; we do not realize ourselves except in contact with others. As Teilhard de Chardin affirms, true union increases one's personal identity. But there is more. Through knowledge and love, we can in a certain sense dwell in one another. One day, a woman who had just lost her son said to me, "For us parents, our children are ourselves." At the level of the family as at the level of all humanity, there is a feeling of solidarity and communion, which makes each self more than itself. Having the same origin and the same end, we all participate in the same divine reality. This profound intuition renders possible a religious detachment, a certain distancing from what we have become, and a decision to abandon oneself to the goodness of life. It empowers us to persevere in self-transcendence and to open ourselves to the whole of reality.

While becoming fully oneself, each person can make a contribution to the world, according to the design of God, which embraces all people. For each of us is more than just one ego; we are what God wants to make of us by locating us in history as irreplaceable agents. Even if some apparently refuse to join in the common movement, that does not

---

[1] The importance of the distinction between ego and self was brought home to me by Sebastian Moore's writings. See Louis Roy, "Human Desire and Easter Faith," in *Jesus Crucified and Risen: Essays in Spirituality and Theology in Honor of Dom Sebastian Moore,* ed. William P. Loewe and Vernon J. Gregson (Collegeville: The Liturgical Press, 1998) 53–66.

prevent God, the master of events, from bringing about a better humanity, through the meanders of their long march.

The Horizon of an Unsuspected Reality   Christian revelation unveils a reality much more vast and sublime than the one envisioned by materialism, and even greater than the one glimpsed by people who are concerned with the best of secular values. That reality, which the New Testament calls the kingdom of God, is equivalent to the final coming together of the human family into the mystery that calls them forward. This reality includes the dimension of the future, of hope, and of the promises of God. For Christians, the coming of God is part of reality. The presence and action of God in time relativize the present moment. On the one hand, they situate it within a long-range movement; on the other hand, they allow us to better enjoy this limited present, a stage on the way to the promised salvation.

Another metaphor, that of the body of Christ (1 Cor 12:12-31), also illustrates this reality. Each Christian is part of the body and concerned about the whole. The interests, values, and goals that polarize the energies of the individual are integrated into the great project—the growth of the body of Jesus Christ. One finds joy, then, in mothering and fathering human beings. "When a woman is in labor, she has pain, because her hour has come. But when her child is born, she no longer remembers the anguish because of the joy of having brought a human being into the world" (John 16:21).

This joy can also be found in caring for the sick and the weak. Just as, in view of the good of the whole, the healthy members of the human body give much attention and care to ill or infirm members, a oneness of destiny leads us to extend to widening circles the kind of care a mother or father spontaneously shows to a child in need.

The reality that Christianity recognizes includes the existence of evil. When self-realization has no religious horizon, it is incapable of dealing with such misfortunes as major disappointments, failures, defeats, humiliations, blows, betrayals, permanent psychic wounds, moral weaknesses, prolonged illness—in short, excessive sufferings that surpass anything that one might possibly gain from them on the human level.

By contrast, far from denying evil, the gospel confronts it directly and offers a practical solution: the Cross. The praxis of Jesus and of believers defeats evil by inspiring acts of generosity, nondefensiveness, and hope, which surpass ordinary wisdom. People who open themselves to reconciliation absorb hatred in their bodies and bring peace (Eph 2:14-17). What St. Paul calls "God's foolishness" proves to be "God's wisdom" (1 Cor 1:18–2:16). In action as in suffering, the Cross sums up and subsumes all that is negative in human existence. In overcoming evil by good, inertia by initiative, and egoism by self-giving, the Cross becomes the unique solution to the problem of evil. It is as much the law of life as the law of Christ. Because of the resurrection, it has an eschatological value. It is the Cross that operates now and will triumph at the end of time.

This vision of faith constitutes the horizon which throws light upon everything else. Whenever standard wisdom loses sight of the example given by Jesus, of the Father's immense love, and of humanity's collective destiny, the radical gospel becomes a scandal. It is the very mystery of God, in fact, that is offered to us. A single mystery of love, self-transcendence, and fullness can be seen in the Trinity as well as in the creative and liberating action of God in which we play a part. Through earthly mediations, and following the lead of Jesus, it is possible for us to leave behind, one by one, various stages of ego development, in order to be taken up into the divine self.[2]

The Gift of Self

It is in this perspective that we can understand the possibility of making a total gift of ourselves. This gift of self goes beyond simple renunciation, which arises from the necessity of making choices. The normal exercise of human freedom implies that an individual chooses a certain good and therefore must set aside another, since she cannot experience everything simultaneously. She cannot concentrate on some good work, for instance, without renouncing other equally worthwhile commitments. Renunciation also relates to her scale of preferences and hierarchy of values. When she gives precedence to a higher good, the pleasure that might have been derived from a lower one is forsaken. This latter form of renunciation can be very demanding. For example, those who are deeply immersed in the gospel must be ready to sacrifice many lesser goods, in order that the Good News may be brought to the poor and divine love may be recognized by as many people as possible.

Even in contexts that are not explicitly religious, people discover in themselves, often with surprise, riches which relativize their daily concerns. They become convinced that generosity does not impoverish. Speaking to Romeo, Juliet exclaims,

> My bounty is as boundless as the sea,
> My love as deep; the more I give to thee
> The more I have, for both are infinite.[3]

[2] On various approaches to this topic, see Louis Roy, *Mystical Consciousness: Western Perspectives and Dialogue with Japanese Thinkers*, SUNY Press, Albany, N.Y., forthcoming.
[3] William Shakespeare, *Romeo and Juliet*, Act 2, Scene 2, verses 133–35.

Aside from certain forms of spontaneous heroism (for example, the mother who throws herself on her child's attacker, or the lifeguard who rushes to the rescue of an imprudent swimmer drawn by threatening sea undertows), human beings cannot consistently endanger their life without reference to an ultimate value, although such a reference may remain unarticulated. How can they sacrifice themselves for an equal if a common destiny does not unite them in an adventure that is greater than them all? It was *to God* that Jesus offered his life at the moment of death: "Father, into your hands I commend my spirit" (Luke 23:46).

Whether we call it the kingdom of God, the body of Christ, the Vine that Jesus is, with us as its branches, the Holy City, the new Jerusalem, Christianity presents a dynamic and transcendent reality, which attracts and surrounds us. At the heart of this reality is the example of Jesus—his way of life, death, and resurrection. We can resolve to transcend ourselves in favor of justice and other human values to the extent that we believe these efforts will not be in vain.

Faith in the resurrection qualifies the pursuit of self-fulfillment. Through the experience of making choices dictated by the highest values of the hierarchy, one becomes aware that the ego does not have to be realized in all its aspects. As Matthew 5:29-30 indicates metaphorically, it is better to accept being deprived of an eye or a hand than to go unmaimed into perdition. This explains Christ's saying, "Those who lose their life for my sake, and for the sake of the gospel, will save it" (Mark 8:35). To lose one's life means to lose a part of one's *ego*, or (in some cases) all of it. But in losing one's life for Christ's sake, one's *self* or one's deepest being is saved, as it is united with God and with all those who belong to the body of Christ.

A purely human motivation of an ethical nature cannot lead a person as far in the gift of self as a religious motivation. The latter is based on discovering God in Jesus:

> Hope does not disappoint us, because God's love has been poured into our hearts through the Holy Spirit that has been given to us. For while we were still weak, at the right time Christ died for the ungodly. Indeed, rarely will anyone die for a righteous person—though perhaps for a good person someone might actually dare to die (Rom 5:5-8).

The experience of having been loved so intensely results in a longing to help others make the same discovery. Having known a God who gives us and wants back the best of our selves, we wish that others will become their best selves. Because we know the signs of hunger for love, we recognize them in the eyes of people we meet. "When he saw the crowds, he had compassion for them, because they were harassed and helpless, like sheep without a shepherd" (Matt 9:36).

Thus we grow in sensitivity and compassion. Our "charity" *(agape)* can become what St. Paul describes in the thirteenth chapter of the first letter to the Corinthians. It does not always have to be emotionally felt in order to be genuine and effective. Whatever the atmosphere surrounding a person, if she is loving, she will not be niggardly in her efforts; she will be generous and self-transcending, because she knows that God is thinking of her. Dazzled by God, she seeks to share with others what she has found to be the best part of life—this God of love. And if she becomes demanding of others, it is because she is persuaded that they, too, ought to grow in love. She recalls the word of Jesus: "It is more blessed to give than to receive" (Acts 20:35).[4]

The Fascination for God

What exactly is the depth of the self that the Cross and the resurrection allow to be saved? It is the most fundamental aspect of human relationships. It is realized by entering into a communion with the Father, the Son, and the Holy Spirit. In realizing it, one finds a priceless treasure worthy of having everything else subordinated to it. "For where your treasure is, there your heart will be too" (Matt 6:21; see 13:44).

Such a centering on God revolutionizes the existence of believers. Communion with God is the keystone of the Christian temple. Only friendship with God can begin to satisfy the human being. Such a relationship explains why the divine Law goes beyond the capacities of human morality. "You shall be holy, for I the Lord your God am holy" (Lev 19:2). This demanding imitation calls for costly sacrifices on the part of believers. Their personalities, marked by sin and the disequilibrium that results from it, cannot easily be integrated into the primacy of the divine. A tension arises between the fascination exercised by this spellbinding God and the limited desires of our daily life.

And yet this fascination must be developed. Unfortunately many Christians have no real interest in God. They think of God only to thank God for creation and to receive his moral help. This stance brings about an ethical conversion, but not a genuine religious conversion. Thus, Christ becomes for them the example and guarantor of what they want to accomplish. Jesus appears as the man who loves life and supports what is human. In that way he reveals something of the Father. But his invitation to become involved with God is not necessarily welcomed by these believers.

[4] On the issue of self-gift, see Louis Roy, "Should Desire Be Consecrated to God?" *The Way* 41 (2001) 157–63.

Does the absence of interest in God deprive believers of something important? Does it prevent them from struggling against their own defects and attaining self-fulfillment? Must one love God with one's whole heart in order to be able to love others in that way? The answer to these questions cannot but be affirmative, because the values that one recognizes as preeminent become idols—idols as noble as one's own personal growth and that of others, or the struggle for more justice and less misery—insofar as the living God does not hold first place in one's life. Fortunately it happens that God makes himself present in the depths of the human heart even if many people cannot give a name to the fascinating mystery which touches them. But lacking religious detachment in the pursuit of their goals, many experience a certain rigidity, which can vitiate their search for these values.

Those who experience the attraction of the infinite Mystery are convinced that God alone is the ultimate good for each person and for the whole human family. Self-realization and success in life cease to be absorbing preoccupations. The ethical commitment remains serious and in fact increases. But self-realization comes to be perceived as already given and assured. That is why one ceases to be excessively concerned with signs of success and becomes more interested in God. From this there arises a definite joy, a harmony in the daily comings and goings, and also great freedom. Interest in God crowns the opening to all of reality. Profound gratitude develops in the person to whom God has manifested his presence.

In this climate of grace, interest in God and gospel radicalism resolutely interact. Speaking of "costly grace,"[5] Dietrich Bonhoeffer emphasizes both the courage demanded of the disciples of Christ and the fact that this courage is given by God. This gift of God is more fundamental than the human response, although the two prove to be inseparable. A reversal of perspective becomes operative as soon as one becomes more attentive to grace than to human effort. In fact, self-transcendence and self-realization are both given by the Holy Spirit.

From this awareness arises an atmosphere of hope and humility, personal peace, and dedication to the work of our vocation. There is therefore no need to be overanxious about our limited attainment of self-transcendence and self-realization. Of course, we must seek ways to foster such attainment. But the best means is by concerning ourselves first with the Father, the source of love; with Jesus, who is our companion; with the Holy Spirit, who inspires us and assumes the responsibility for making a success of our life; and with the people

---

[5] Dietrich Bonhoeffer, *The Cost of Discipleship* (New York: Macmillan, 1963), ch. 1, §1.

around us, including their values, their needs, and their objective appeals directed toward us.

Happiness and Finitude

To experience this interest in God with full authenticity, one must renounce happiness. "Happiness" here refers to the kind of security and plenitude enjoyed in the mother's womb before birth. As soon as we are born, we enter into a process in which we must deal with expectations and frustrations. To accept the limits of reality proves difficult emotionally. That is why people remain nostalgic for the uncomplicated state symbolized by the mother's womb or by a romanticized image of childhood. In adolescents and immature adults, the pursuit of this unattainable goal sometimes becomes intense. Nothing is more disappointing and destructive, for example, than a love experience based on the search for that kind of happiness. The more one wants it, the less one will find it.

This happiness in the strict sense, which we should renounce, differs from happiness in the broad sense. The latter, in fact, is equivalent to the pleasure, satisfaction, joy, or peace that accompanies activities which are interesting, meaningful, and affectively fulfilling. In the measure in which people take a genuine interest in their surroundings, they have this positive experience. It would be foolish to deprive oneself of this happiness, since religious maturity entails it. In contrast to the illusory happiness that certain adults childishly pursue, the happiness we are talking about has nothing exalted about it. And yet, how rewarding it is! When we welcome the personal presence of God and of the kingdom in which he gathers all those who try to love, we cannot but taste that incomparable peace, "not . . . as the world gives" (John 14:27) and that lasting joy of which Jesus says, "no one will take your joy from you" (John 16:22).

But why should we renounce happiness understood in the strict sense? It is because this happiness can only take the form of an idol, that is to say, a limited reality of which we ask a somewhat infinite good. And behind all the idols in which we could place our hope, we find the principal idol, the ego. Is it not the ego that we deify when engaging in activities from which we expect total happiness? Still, we know that neither the ego nor anything in this world is infinite. The ego cannot therefore satisfy itself and it cannot be satisfied by anything finite. In this respect, the myth of unlimited potential, which certain psychologists invite us to actualize, proves deceptive; it usually sponsors changes in our relationships, lifestyle, or career that promise too much and thus inevitably end up in disappointment. Moreover, each time we absolutize the ego, we run the risk of hurting others, since we lose the freedom that allows unconditional respect for them. Idolatry, in fact, renders impossible the detachment and courage that are required to love wholeheartedly.

Gospel radicalism becomes possible when we give up the childish notion of happiness as an immediate totality. We then accept frustrations and suffering, make choices, and realize limited goals. We pursue important values in a realistic fashion, taking successes and failures in stride. We accept our finiteness.

Renouncing happiness does not imply giving up one's love of life. If the Christian mystic lays aside his childish aspirations and abandons the search for a lost paradise, it is not in order to become a stoic. Far from resigning himself to what finite reality offers, he has discovered, on the contrary, a much broader and higher reality. The true adult turns his back on a paradise of the past and goes forward toward the one that lies ahead. What is the difference between these two attitudes? The search for a past paradise consists in trying to transform the finite into the infinite. Openness to the future paradise consists in accepting totally the finitude of our earthly life, viewing it against the horizon of the infinite. Without denying finitude, we welcome a gift of God which comes to us precisely through the finite. The very life of God is given to human beings through Jesus, who experienced finitude:

> Though he was in the form of God, he did not regard equality with God as something to be exploited, but emptied himself, taking the form of a slave, being born in human likeness. And being found in human form, he humbled himself and became obedient to the point of death—even death on a cross. Therefore God also highly exalted him and gave him the name that is above every name, so that at the name of Jesus every knee should bend, in heaven and on earth and under the earth, and every tongue should confess that Jesus Christ is Lord, to the glory of God the Father (Phil 2:6-11).

Chapter 7

Rhythms and Readjustments

How can we take seriously the radicalism of the gospel while being also concerned with our own personal development? This question raises problems about implementation. Let us therefore examine and discuss the rhythms, stages, and elements that contribute to advancement.

Complementary Rhythms

Living beings function according to rhythms. It is unhealthy to want to act always with maximum intensity or to seek continuous comfort. The book of Ecclesiastes wisely emphasizes the importance of respecting the alternating rhythms of major human experiences. Qoheleth states:

> For everything there is a season, and a time for every matter under heaven: a time to be born, and a time to die; . . . a time to weep, and a time to laugh; . . . a time to seek, and a time to lose; a time to keep, and a time to throw away; . . . a time to love, and a time to hate; a time for war, and a time for peace (3:1-8).

Let us recall what was said in chapter 3. When the radical gospel directs human intentionality toward a supreme reality, the principle of limitation, which is the psyche, must balance out this forward movement with periods of rest and recuperation. Otherwise the Christian ideal would become infected with megalomania or other mental illnesses. As a matter of fact, the saints tempered their austerities with activities that brought them a good deal of satisfaction. Unfortunately hagiography has rarely noted this aspect of their wisdom. Unlike materialists, however, the saints did not suffer from an excess of leisure. They both realized and transcended themselves by concentrating on the highest values.

In chapter 3, we considered Maslow's principle that we should not be dependent on categories of exclusion when we think of the relationships between personal needs and interest in the outside world. Instead, his principle favors thinking according to a hierarchical integration. We must now draw the practical conclusion and envision life as alternating between complementary rhythms. These rhythms are many: prayer/commitment, solitude/solidarity, giving/receiving, being with/being for, leisure/work, and so forth.

In this regard, nothing is more treacherous than certain pseudo-universal principles, which transform into absolutes what cannot actually be more than partial aims. Here are some examples: "You have to think of yourself in the first place. You cannot be at ease with other people unless you begin by feeling good about yourself. Self-transcendence supposes that you have first achieved self-actualization. Be autonomous, be yourself, and if that offends others, so much the worse for them. Having to adjust to you cannot but benefit them in the long run." Such maxims support the quest for self-fulfillment.

Here are a few more, this time on the side of self-transcendence: "There is no use in forcing yourself into self-actualization; it is better not to cultivate it, but to take everything simply and to get interested in what lies around you, without introspection. Avoid being subjective; only pay attention to the objective needs of others. The group is more important than the individual. Only take care to love and give constantly—that is the key to happiness. Trust people and they will become honest and generous."

The common defect in all these maxims is that they are excessive in their generality, which makes them exercise an impoverishing effect on those who attempt to apply them. Although many psychologists and preachers serve up such naive pronouncements, experience teaches us that matters are not so simple. Several of these mottos are based on a false temporal or ontological priority: *first* this or that. Thus they claim that individualism must come *before* altruism, or vice versa; or that subjectivity ought to be placed *over* objectivity, or vice versa. Such banalities consider only one side of the coin. In contrast to this one-sidedness, a wise man like Jesus recognizes the healthy tension that must exist between two complementary attitudes: "Be wise as serpents and innocent as doves" (Matt 10:16). He not only says, "Peace I leave with you, my peace I give to you" (John 14:27), but also, "Do not think that I have come to bring peace to the earth; I have not come to bring peace, but a sword" (Matt 10:34).

Alternation is not a mere compromise between the pursuit of happiness and self-abnegation. Instead, one thinks of oneself in order to be able to think of others. To take time for oneself, to rest and relax, to renew one's motivation and energies, to introduce some changes—all that can foster joyful, inventive, and well-adjusted commitment. Can one love another, with real interest in the other, and at the same time have in view one's self-realization? Purists would say no. And yet these two intentions can be united in a movement of coming and going, where one's attention is directed by turns toward the self and toward the other. Thomas Aquinas considered it as natural to love oneself as to be concerned for others and to wish them well:

> The love that a man has for others arises in man from the love that he has for himself, for a man stands in relation to such a friend as he does to himself. But a person loves himself inasmuch as he wishes the good for himself, just as he loves another person by wishing him good. So, by the fact that a man is interested in his own good he is led to develop an interest in another person's good. Hence, because a person hopes for good from some other person, a way develops for man to love that other person in himself, from whom he hopes to attain the good. Indeed, a person is loved in himself when the lover wishes the good for him, even if the lover may receive nothing from him.[1]

If there is a problem, it is that people do not naturally love others right away. They must come to a standstill, reflect, pray and open themselves to the grace of God, in order to learn how to love and act harmoniously.

Far from suppressing the hierarchy of values, the law of alternation allows one to interpret the hierarchy dynamically. Any concrete application requires discernment. A superior value generally (though not always) takes precedence over a lesser value. For example, although pastoral work is obviously more noble than leisure, those who are engaged in the ministry must take time off for relaxation at regular intervals, even if important work is waiting to be done. On the other hand, when an emergency arises, good pastors spontaneously realize that their leisure must be sacrificed.

Part of discernment consists in taking note of what suits various people and circumstances. The gospel commands that either directly or indirectly we should make common cause with the poor, the underserved, and the despised. This supposes a disinterested love, since we are unlikely to get back as much as we give. But this commitment needs to be supported by reciprocal love, either in the same environment (when we receive some gratitude) or in another setting. Thus, when Jesus saw the disciples returning from their preaching, he said to

---

[1] Thomas Aquinas, *Summa Contra Gentiles* (South Bend, Ind.: University of Notre Dame Press, 1975) Book III, ch. 153.

them, "Come away to a deserted place all by yourselves and rest a while" (Mark 6:31).

In the same way, courageous parents can show self-sacrificial love toward a handicapped child born to them, or to an emotionally abused child they have adopted. Or again, a married person can decide to remain with an unfaithful or very difficult partner. Others devote themselves as psychiatrists, psychologists, or nurses, taking care of psychotics and neurotics, or the sick, infirm, or dying. All these forms of radicalism can only be sustained by periods of rest or leisure, during which strength is restored.

Readjustments and Reorientations

In addition to the alternations of complementary rhythms, life causes us to pass through various phases, during which we need to take new bearings. It then becomes important to adjust our ideas, reactions, attitudes or ways of acting, and to redirect our commitments and priorities, sometimes even to the extent of reinterpreting our ultimate goals. These periods of adjustment can prove very difficult. Having inherited from their grandparents a wisdom fashioned in the stable circumstances of an agricultural world, many people have not yet found the wisdom to live without disturbance amid the changes taking place with increasing frequency in the present world.

Traditionally, the criteria of goodness were by and large extrinsic. Most of the time, individual action was evaluated according to the yardstick of a group's principles, moral laws, and customs. In the twentieth century, however, the immense scope of contradictory ideas passed down by education and the mass media has caused the pendulum to swing to the other extreme, to subjectivism. The sphere of action has become psychologized, in the sense that it has become almost entirely subject to premoral considerations, as was explained in chapter 2.

In order to face up to the challenges presented by the various ages and stages of life, and to handle the crises caused by unavoidable circumstances, an individual must develop the ability to change. That supposes that he has a vision that places mobility ahead of immobility. It is not easy to practice fidelity through continual readjustment. It is often easier to transcend ourselves in a setting we have chosen than to become aware of what lies deeply buried in us, to bring to consciousness ambiguous and unsettling material, and thus allow new possibilities of self-transcendence to emerge.

It is important to pay attention to the symptoms indicating that such a review is necessary. A person may feel weary, dissatisfied, less and less motivated, anxious, vaguely guilty, or depressed without any particular reason—in short, she has ceased to function as she used before and she no longer understands herself. Dwelling on these symptoms will normally lessen her commitment. And yet, if radicalism implies forward movement, she must state frankly that it is more gospel-like to recognize that she is in a questioning period, and then seek out help toward a clearer understanding of her position.

What is radical, then, is to accept oneself with one's ambiguities. To be a pilgrim is to enter resolutely into the crisis, with the courage to face uncertainty and risk, and to confront doubts, regrets, fears, and complex problems. It is noble to arrive at the truth regarding one's real feelings, to unmask negative tendencies, to become more familiar with one's fantasies, desires, sexuality, and mode of relating to others—in sum, to accept all such psychic experience and to integrate it into one's consciousness.

Some people feel guilty if they give up certain outlooks and options that have always been linked to a religious ideal. Other people are disturbed to discover their need to abandon viewpoints or preferences that were based on a superficial understanding of self-realization. When self-transcendence and self-actualization are misunderstood, it is hard to admit that our former way of seeing and choosing is no longer suited to what we have become or are called to become. Let us think of the Pharisee Paul, who had to renounce his legalistic past: "Forgetting what lies behind and straining forward to what lies ahead, I press on toward the goal" (Phil 3:13-14).

The danger to be avoided here is the cultivation, in the name of the gospel, of childishness in oneself or in others. Passages in the New Testament dealing with radical demands can appear to be invitations to a false self-denial for people who are weak or in crisis. What belongs to a supramoral context may serve to support action of a inframoral kind. In this case, far from promoting personal growth, the religious ideal only contributes to the psychological stagnation of the individual who clings to a false notion of this ideal. Unfortunately, the great Christian values can encourage attitudes of ill-considered devotion, submission to others, and self-annihilation before God.

Various phenomena then take place. A long period of frustration often induces fascination with the things we have always secretly desired. In the handling of possessions, leisure, or sexuality, we may become obsessed by the images of objects, pleasures, or experiences that we have been denied. Regrets concerning what we missed in the past may lead to the kind of lust for experiences which was described in chapter 2.

It can be the same with self-actualization: too long neglected, it may suddenly be perceived as a sacred right, a matter of urgency, which is then striven after in an unsuitable way. In this case, the compulsion toward self-indulgence reduces other people to mere objects to be grasped and enjoyed.

Moreover, apart from this type of fascination and obsession, one can also experience the phenomenon of "indigestion," wherein one rejects whatever was excessive, imposed, or badly understood in the restrictive practices of the past. Or again, there may be regression when one's ethical system breaks apart and disintegrates.

We must not telescope this disturbing phase of human development. It would be artificial and unhealthy to stifle the appeals of the unconscious, to silence questions, and to continue as before, trying to maintain a spurious ideal of self-transcendence. During this phase, in fact, the gift of self is practically impossible, because the self that is to be given has been so weakened that it is virtually void. This is not the time to pose any challenge other than facing one's problems. Instead, time has come to examine oneself, heal one's wounds, and renew oneself.

The same wisdom is required when a system of egotistical principles crumbles. One should not immediately and rigorously put forward the contrary ideal of self-transcendence. Again, the individual in this case has no true self to give. If he prematurely embraces the idea of self-giving, he will try to carry it out with the same clumsiness that characterized his search for individual happiness. He will easily become intoxicated by the illusion of his recent generosity. While applauding his efforts to take into consideration the good of others, it is important to allow him no longer to concentrate on performance, but to open himself to a much needed personal transformation which is a matter more of grace than of striving.

Counseling or therapy can help enormously, provided that the counselor respects the moral and religious dimensions of the person. A psychological readjustment, if well done, can lead to reorientations of the moral and religious order. In the same way, spiritual direction allows links to be established between the psychomoral modifications that are taking place and the Christian meaning of one's journey. The presence of a good listener helps the person to interiorize the fact that God sees with love and compassion all that the human being has within herself. Hope on the part of the therapist or spiritual guide plays a very significant role. It is not easy to let go of abnormalities in the line of either self-transcendence or of self-actualization. To admit that she has attributed a false value to oneself is risky; it can diminish her self-esteem and can cause depression, discouragement, and sometimes despair. It is important, therefore, that the discovery of negative aspects coincides with a discovery of positive aspects. The listener should help the person to find beauty in herself.

The Psychic, the Social, and the Spiritual

The development of the human being requires the interaction of three fundamental dimensions: the psychic, the social, and the spiritual. In the 1960s, a good number of psychologists who were writing about self-actualization paid little attention to the social context. Because of this lacuna, today their fine theories look rather removed from real life. Coming before the economic recession of the late seventies, the atmosphere of that time was optimistic: everything seemed possible in the West. But the mood has changed. Statistics show that since the 1980s, even in rich countries the buying power of the majority of the population has slowly decreased. This factor makes the superficial pursuit of self-actualization more difficult. As the price of apartments, hotels, restaurants, travel, vacation spots, etc., has been steadily increasing, being unfaithful to one's partner or arranging a divorce has become more and more expensive, especially for those with children.

Even though the revenues of the middle class have improved in the 1990s, psychological issues need to be related to other phenomena which affect collectivities. For the last two decades or so, some authors have placed the ideal of self-realization within its real social and economic setting.[2] Certain psychologists have insisted that problems within the home arise in large part from unhealthy tensions and dissatisfactions at work. The job itself may be insignificant or mere routine. Moreover, interpersonal relations at work are generally insipid, sometimes difficult, and seldom satisfying. Finally, it is not always evident to the workers how they are contributing to the general good of society. On each of these points, a Christian vision of life, coupled with some psychological knowledge, can enable a person to find a situation that allows for more initiative, patience, and hope. When one discovers in faith a reason for living as well as profound peace, and when one is capable of relating to others with serenity and humor, with self-respect and esteem for them, then one is able to recognize what work can and cannot give, and one discerns what may be changed now and what may perhaps be changed later.

One area where many readjustments are needed consists in relationships between men and women. The numerous problems on which feminist writings inform us must be heard, reflected upon, and treated with tact. For a married couple, the division of work should not be immutable. Kindness, empathy, a critical mind, a capacity for confrontation and negotiation must be present if people are going to make good

---

[2] For example, Daniel Yankelovich, *New Rules* (New York: Random House, 1981).

decisions about such questions as the following: What friends and social contacts will we choose? How much contact will we have with our
respective families? How many children will we have, and when? What
are our priorities for allocating our money? If both of us get promising
job offers in different cities, which one shall we accept? If one of us
wishes to pursue a degree, will the other be the sole support? In dis-
cussing these problems, the partners must be careful that the religious
motivation of self-transcendence does not make them lose sight of the
psychological dimension.

One must also make room for initiatives and creativity at home as
well as in other settings. In democratic societies, there are many volun-
tary associations directed toward widely different objectives. Christians should encourage one another to recognize the importance of
such commitments and to find those that suit them. Aside from its intrinsic value, a commitment to church or society that makes the best
use of someone's talents can do much to balance family life and work.

A willingness to be involved with others will contribute much in the
effort to achieve self-actualization in an evangelical perspective. Passivity is fatal. When people perceive that they have practically nothing
to say either about the organization of their work or about society in
general, their interest flows back into their private life. What they
vaguely know and yet are reluctant to admit is that even their private
life is largely regulated from outside. Alienation in regard to the environment thus ensues. Whether alone or in a group, these people isolate
themselves in superficial pastimes or other experiences. Unfortunately,
counselors and psychotherapists often do little to sensitize their clients
to the social dimensions of their problems. Being too readily willing
themselves to accept society's rules—which they mistake for "reality"—they do not help their clients go against the dominant disvalues.
In the prevailing relativism, even true values are seen only as a means
to individualistic self-realization. The slogan is: "If pursuing that particular value makes you happy, go ahead with it!"

Michael Lerner denounces the powerlessness that affects a large part
of the American public in the face of deplorable conditions in their society.[3] He finds that the ideology of "meritocracy" blames individuals
for their problems. Denying the economic, social, and political causes
of these problems, this ideology makes people believe that it is up to
the individuals only to fulfill themselves. Consequently, solutions to
their difficulties are sought through improved health, sports, or atti-

---

[3] Michael Lerner, *Surplus Powerlessness* (Atlantic Highlands, N.J.: Humanities
Press, 1991).

tude changes brought about in small groups. There is no recognition of the fact that frustration arises from the lack of change in the economy.

Lerner calls "surplus powerlessness" the belief that ordinary people who are dissatisfied with society can do nothing to change it fundamentally. People have let themselves be convinced that human nature is essentially egotistical, self-interested, and eager to succeed at the expense of others. Not expecting any true solidarity from their fellow citizens, they conclude that they are bound to remain passive and let the financial and political elite control money, the mass media, and public opinion. They are convinced that, despite all their efforts, defeat is inevitable. When people are really sure that they do not deserve success, they resign themselves to be losers, so that they can continue to blame and denigrate themselves and others.

Such is the prophetic analysis presented by Lerner. After the sociopolitical disappointments of the late sixties, he gave up teaching philosophy in a university, obtained his doctorate in clinical psychology, and joined a group of psychiatrists, psychologists, social workers, family therapists, labor leaders, and activists to form an institute for reflection and psychosocial action. He is typical of a minority in wealthy countries, continuing to think freely and to discuss strategies that might promote interaction among the psychic, the social, and the spiritual.

Lerner preaches the renunciation of riches, security and reputation gained at others' expense, and the rejection of the ideology of powerlessness. He urges a renewal of hope with the help of the great religious traditions of humankind. He suggests that authentic communities be created, where people learn to listen, to dialogue, to respect one another, to accept imperfection, to understand common problems, and to be anxious that the group progress together as human beings. Finally, he welcomes initiatives toward collaboration with other groups, and he hopes that this kind of activity will, in time, generate a mass movement.

This chapter has emphasized rhythms, readjustments, as well as interactions between the psychic, the social, and the spiritual in the process of self-actualization. The above example illustrates the reemergence of values close to gospel radicalism in a milieu where one would perhaps not expect to find them. This says much about the action of the Holy Spirit in our world.

Conclusion

In the course of this undertaking, a double conviction has propelled us: living faith is both inculturated and countercultural. Notice how the following two texts taken from St. Paul's letters balance each other.

> Whatever is true, whatever is honorable, whatever is just, whatever is pure, whatever is pleasing, whatever is commendable, if there is any excellence and if there is anything worthy of praise, think about these things (Phil 4:8).

> Do not be conformed to this world, but be transformed by the renewing of your minds, so that you may discern what is the will of God—what is good and acceptable and perfect (Rom 12:2).

The gospel is transformative of culture, not by merely adapting itself to it, but through sifting, purifying, and strengthening the valuable components of that culture. In our contemporary world, one of the paramount values is self-actualization. Accordingly the issue that we have tackled has been, how can we be inculturated and countercultural *in a discerning manner*?

In this inquiry, we looked for a concept that would help us establish connections between the various aspects of the problem under discussion. The human openness to reality has been this operative linchpin. In analyzing defective forms of self-transcendence and of self-actualization, the first two chapters have shown that those shortcomings derive from a lack of respect for the reality of the acting subject and for the reality of others. Chapter 3 has drawn attention to the intentionality in the depths of human nature, namely, the capacity to be open to and interested in reality, especially interpersonal and social reality. Our desire to know and love raises questions and leads to acts that promote what is truly good. In chapters 4 and 5, we have listened to radical texts of the New

Testament that urge us to acknowledge a reality infinitely more vast and noble than any goal envisaged by ordinary human wisdom. This reality is called the kingdom of God, that is, what God wants to actualize among human beings.

Thanks to this opening up to reality, chapter 6 has established that despite the fact that self-actualization and the radical gospel do clash with one another in a great number of instances, a synthesis is not only desirable but also possible in the lives of people who respond to divine grace. However, this synthesis cannot take place purely on the basis of the human tendency toward self-actualization. Instead, it is the Christian vision of life that must integrate the tendency toward self-actualization into a larger drama. The process of integration requires that the drive toward self-realization be deep and critical enough to recognize its own deviations, while accentuating its strengths and welcoming meaning and values that shift it into a richer context. In chapter 7, we have illustrated various difficulties to be taken account of in the journey toward a fuller and more satisfying unification.

The decisive attitude consists in gratefully receiving our fulfillment from our loving Creator, either through human mediations or in prayerful immediacy. We experience deep joy provided we accept the fact that our self-actualization remains partial. We can then take in stride the inevitable alternation of ups and downs, of progress and crisis, of temporary stagnation followed by fresh starts. Throughout the unique itinerary which constitutes our life, it is up to each of us to find our own forms of gospel radicalism, as we are attentive to the needs of others, to our personal gifts, and to the voice of the Holy Spirit.

Index